Magi Adoration

To Margaret & Eddy
At one time our' neighbours
from heaven.
I'm sure you will enjoy
my latest scribbling
as you journey with
the MAGI.
Love & Godbless
George Crawford
2015.

Magi Adoration

An embellishment to Christmas

George Cornford

Published by www.lulu.com

Quotes introducing stages along the journey from the timeless old carols:
Hark the herald-angels sing. Charles Wesley 1707-1780
Angels from the realms of glory. James Montgomery 1771-1854
Brightest and best are the sons of the morning. Reginald Heber 1783-1826

MAGI ADORATION

ISBN 978-1-326-29958-3

Book formatted by www.bookformatting.co.uk.

Contents

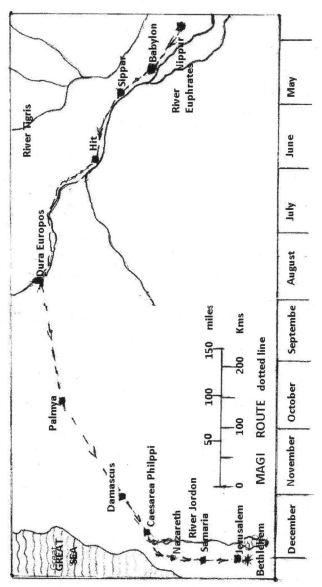

The new star cluster was seen at Babylon and led them along from
West to East. Months relate to position of star cluster.

East to West

Map of the middle east not to scale.
It shows the route taken by the Magi.

About this book

Go with the Magi as they take the reader on a journey from Babylon to Bethlehem in order to fulfil their part in the Adoration of The Christ Child.

Astronomy was one of the most important sciences during the first century BC. it had been so for thousands of years.

Men who studied it were soought after by rulers and monarchs in order to assist in governing their countries.

This story explains how they could have found any new stars, the equipment they would have used during that period of time, and the environment they worked and studied in.

Long before the time of Jesus, Greek scholars had become well advanced in all the sciences.

Over one thousand stars had been plotted and named, years had been divided into months, weeks, days and hours, using the base number of sixty.

When the Magi discover the new stars they are compelled to travel on a journey of a lifetime as if by a calling they cannot explain.

They are encouraged along by prophesies from the Old Testament Scriptures.

When they finally meet and worship the King of Kings their lives are transformed forever.

Written for all who love Christmas.

Prologue

The story of the Magi is a favourite part of Christmas.

Every year we look forward to watching three children with cardboard crowns dressed as kings enacting the visit and Adoration of the Christ Child as they lay their gifts before a doll or occasionally a baby.

Within minutes it is all over and done with until the following year.

The fact that it really happened is recorded by St. Matthew in the second chapter of his Gospel.

It is a very brief account and does not give a name of even one of the Wise Men, or where they came from, or how many there were.

It is assumed there were three because of the three gifts.

According to which translation we read, they were called Wise Men or Magi.

The Greeks called wise men who studied the stars Magi.

It was also the title of Persian priests and we know they were Astronomers. Matthew does record they did follow a star from the east.

Astronomy had been studied well over two thousand years by the time Jesus was born, most Kings and Rulers had a group of such men around them to help and advise them how to govern the country, that proves they were held in high esteem.

I decided to study and research with a view of trying to uncover what sort of men the Magi might have been and where they may have come from.

Academies had been available for students in many parts of the known world, Greek scholars had made such advanced strides in mathematics, astronomy, physics and all the sciences, it is obvious their learning complexes must have been among the best available.

One of their great Academies of Astronomy was at Alexandria. By the time of the Magi's visit it was already an acclaimed learning complex of renown and had been in use for centuries.

Academics of distinction studied and taught there themselves.

My research gave me the inspiration to write this story of how such men could have been called from so far away and led to where the Messiah was born.

Using names taken from various parts of the bible, I decided to create four characters, one of whom had a biblical background to advise them.

It reminded me of the Book of Daniel where four Jewish students were taken by Nebuchadnezzar to Babylon and educated with a view to work in the Babylonian government.

And so about the year 32 BC my four fictitious students were enrolled to study at the Alexandria Academy, where they studied and became Magi of repute.

During this time together, they developed a friendship between them bonding them almost like brothers.

They each came from a different country, but all were from wealthy families of standing.

They were Merchant Princes.

Not as great Kings such as Darius or Nebuchadnezzar, more like the standing of our Barons and Dukes.

Kings of the Yemen, and most countries around the Middle East had adopted the Jewish faith by 120 BC.

This would have given rise to most of them knowing that the Jews had been expecting a Messiah for many years by the time the story unfolds.

Each character has been given a biblical name that has a bearing to the country of his origin.

They travelled in the northern hemisphere and the way the earth revolves brings the sun and stars from east to west, thus to follow a star one had to travel westwards.

Telescopes were not invented until the time of Galileo.

So all who studied the stars would need a strong pair of eyes.

The instrument they would have used would have been the Greek dioptra, or the Arabic alidade.

This device comprised of a length of metal about 30 cm., with vanes or rings fixed at each end, which in turn were fixed to metal circles divided into units around the perimeter to give measurements of angles and direction.

Hipparcus, the famous Greek Astronomer had developed this well over a hundred years previous.

He had plotted and recorded over a thousand stars, his catalogue was used for centuries after his time.

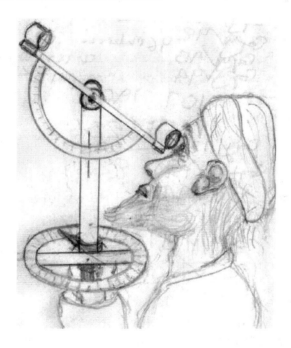

DIOPTRA

The circle had been divided into 360 degrees, days into 24 hours.

A year into 365 days.

With their position being nearer the equator, it meant that the position of the stars had moved slightly more than one degree from one night to the next.

The dioptra may seem a sophisticated piece of equipment for them to use in 6 BC.

However, to prove that astronomers and indeed geographers were so advanced, in 1900 a wrecked ship was discovered off the Greek Island of Antikythera by a team of sponge divers.

Among the wreckage was a piece of machinery with over thirty gears. It was made of a non-ferrous metal.

When scientists studied it, it caused quite a stir, especially among the Astronomers.

Even now it is classed as a very significant find.

Present day astronomers have made replicas of the find that caused such a sensation.

We now believe that it is the worlds first analogue computer made by Greek engineers sometime around 100 BC.

By turning a central gear it could predict where the sun, moon and planets would be on any given date.

It is known as the Nama Machine, and now resides in the Athens Museum.

The Greeks brought a much more civilised way of life to the middle east which was accepted by most countries invaded by Alexander.

Even the Jews in Judea now spoke Greek.

However, after the Jewish Exile, the larger Jewish Community that settled between the two great rivers, Euphrates and Tigris, continued to speak Hebrew.

Although this part of the Christmas story is called Epiphany, held by the Church on January 6th, most scholars today believe the Magi's visit was not until much later, perhaps twelve months or so after the Birth of Jesus.

The two instances pointing to this are where the
Bible states 'where is He born to be King',
also 'on coming to the house', not a 'stable'.

My research with the stars was done using a Planisphere.

This predicts how and when stars rise and fall.

From this I placed the imaginary stars in Leo Minor to rise in early May and fall in the following December.

Obviously this is all surmised but I have endeavoured to tie in with all the facts recorded in St. Matthews Gospel.

Wherever the Scriptures are quoted they are taken mostly from the NIV unless otherwise stated.

ONLY BIBLE REFERENCES SHOULD BE TAKEN AS TRUE FACTS.

The rest of the story is my fictitious attempt to give a background to a group of 'Magi' who would follow a star, to seek and find, and bear gifts to honour The King of Kings.

The story begins in the year 6 BC.

Most scholars today believe the actual date of Jesus' Birth was between 6 and 5 BC.

Babylon

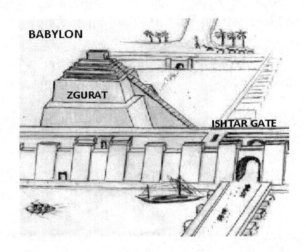

Sages, leave your contemplations, Brighter visions beam afar.
Seek the great Desire of nations; Ye have seen His natal star.
(J Montgomery)

Kedar was studying the Constellation of Leo.

Whatever prompted him to look in that part of the sky just at that moment he'll never know.

But somehow he fixed his gaze on a few tiny stars that were so dim they could only just be seen with the naked eye.

The instrument he was looking through was a dioptra.

Kedar had focused on these dim stars for a few minutes and slowly realised they were not plotted on his chart.

"Meres, what do you make of this"?

"What are you looking at"? came the reply.

"Focus on Leo and find Regulas" directed Kedar.

Regulas was one of the brightest stars in the Constellation of Leo.

These stars were the ones just coming into view in the eastern sky, some of which would be seen during the next year cycle as they moved through the sky from east to west.

It took a few minutes for Meres to set his dioptra to the new position.

He found Regulas, a few moments later he shouted,

"Wow, I see what you've found".

"I'm not imagining it then am I"? Kedar almost shouted excitedly, then added,

"What do you see"?

"I'm sure there are three small stars making a triangle" answered Meres.

"That's just what I see", Kedar answered.

"You could study for years and not find them, you are lucky Kedar, you could have stars named after you".

Neither of them spoke for the next few minutes, they were so engrossed in the new discovery.

Their equipment had been set up on one of the brick observation platforms built in this ancient city of Babylon.

It was old even before the time of Abraham.

Kedar and Meres each had a servant and a bodyguard that travelled with them at all times, the reason being Kedar and Meres were Royal Princes.

Each person rode a camel, two more for pack animals in order for the Royal Party to travel in style.

The servants and bodyguards were also well educated and realised their Royal Masters were very excited about something they had observed.

One of them called out,

"Do you want us to record your finds, Prince Kedar"?

"Yes Midian" replied Kedar,

"Be as accurate as you can, we will check when you have plotted it".

Each assistant knew just how to observe the sky, so when they saw the new stars for themselves they realised why the Princes were so excited.

A pot lantern was placed near enough for Kedar to work with.

A new parchment was placed by the side of the star chart.

Regulas and the other stars in Leo were drawn on the new parchment and given to Kedar.

He carefully put the new stars in one by one, as he looked first through his dioptra and back to the chart.

Meres checked and agreed.

"Midian, you double check the position, all of you see if you agree, we could have a very important find".

There was a sound of excitement in Kedar's voice.

From this old observation platform they could look around the ancient City of Babylon.

A full moon gave an eerie glow to the great brick monuments, parts of their ruins can still be seen today.

Babylon was built on the eastern side of the Great River Euphrates. As they looked westward they could pick out all the prominent structures showing the architectural beauty seen clearly by the light of the moon.

Hot sun, river-water, and clay were very plentiful.

A building project of gigantic proportion had been undertaken by the Babylonians, part of which, the Hanging Gardens, were to the Greeks, one of the Seven Wonders of the World.

A great bridge had been built across the river leading into the City, through the Great Archway of a double wall.

A moat ran between the two great walls that surrounded the city.

This archway was called the Ishtar Gate, named after the Babylonian god.

Glazed kiln dried bricks were produced to give a finished surface to the whole facade which depicted large coloured frescos of local flora and fauna.

Today, parts of these structures can be seen in museums, taken by western archaeologists who first explored and excavated these ancient sites.

Babylon the Great was now very much a disused site apart from Bedouins and a few settlements of displaced people owing to the many upheavals and disruptions the local people had endured as great warring nations came and went.

As the apparatus was taken down from the viewing platform, Kedar and Meres were trying to come to terms with this great new find.

Hardly a word had been spoken since the recording.

Then Meres had a thought and shouted,

"We must go and tell King Shadrach of your find".

Kedar replied immediately,

"Yes, – I wondered if you'd think that way too".

Meres grinned as he said,

"He will be delighted with such a find, I'll tell Midian we will move with the dawn to Sippar.

Midian was his personal attendant.

Sippar lay thirty miles to the north, it was another ancient City but not as important as Babylon had once been.

Several of these ancient cities became less important as and when the great river changed its course.

King Shadrach lived on a large estate in Sippar.

He was the Tribal King of a highly respected Babylonian Dynasty, the Egibi Family.

They were the Rothchilds of the day, members of most of the Merchant Syndicates.

Like most Royal Lineages, he had a family line that could be traced back many centuries to famous Astronomer Advisors that Nebuchadnezzar, Darius and other Persian kings had used to advise them.

A large convention of Astronomers had met in Nippur three weeks earlier, and Shadrach, being in his eighties was the most senior Magi.

He had been the Guest of Honour.

Kedar and Meres had also attended the gathering accompanied

by two of their colleagues, Ashpenaze and Joiada.

Over twenty five years earlier, the four of them had studied at the School of Alexandria as students.

Each one of them had been awarded the covetous Time-Star.

During that five year period of studying together, they had formed a brotherhood bond that would last a lifetime.

Their greatest connection being, each was a Royal Prince.

Ashpenaz was also nephew and heir to King Shadrach.

King Shadrach's Estate, Sippar.

Star of the East, the horizon adorning,
Guide where our Infant Redeemer is laid.
(R Heber)

After two days steady travel they were approaching Shadrach's palatial family home.

To the locals it seemed as if it had been there for ever, some of their families had worked on the Estate for generations.

They rode by a large building that was well known to travellers.

A large sign invited people of any race, be they rich or poor, to have a welcome rest with refreshments.

Kedar and Meres turned into the large gated entrance beyond and rode along the well maintained path that led through olive groves, vineyards and palm trees.

A mile further on they were greeted by the head of the large community of servants.

The two Royal Visitors had been recognised and King Shadrach was already on his way to the reception area.

"May you both live for ever my two young Princes. Something very important must have brought you to my humble dwelling".

Shadrach's greeting could be heard quite clearly as they passed through the large aperture of the perimeter wall into the paved quadrangle.

The ornate fountain could be heard splashing into the palm-shaded pond, where coloured carp glinted in the afternoon sunshine.

The princes each bowed to their royal host before taking turns to embrace him.

"My Lord Shadrach" replied Meres,

"Kedar has found something very special".

"Has he indeed"? exclaimed the King.

He looked up into the sky and with a twinkle in his eye and quietly followed with,

"It must be in the stars".

"Is it that obvious" answered Kedar, "But you always seem to have a notion if it concerns the stars".

"You will go and refresh yourselves and join me for refreshments, we will have an early meal in order to study the stars. Then you can tell me all about it".

Servants attended them showing the way to a sumptuous guest room that could have been found in 'The Arabian Nights'.

Two hours later they were reclining around a low table that was literally laid for Royalty.

Nothing had been spared.

Meres began to explain their visit to King Shadrach.

"After leaving the convention, Kedar and myself decided to call at the old observation site in Babylon".

"To enjoy the pleasure of a night of stargazing can only be appreciated by such beings as ourselves" declared Shadrach, and then added,

"Kedar has spotted something unusual"?

He looked at Kedar as he spoke.

"I could not believe what I saw, at first I thought my eyes were playing tricks, I told Meres where to look. When he described exactly what I was looking at, I was even more mystified, I still think it must be a dream".

"It's no dream my Lord Shadrach, I can't wait for your reaction when the sun goes down" Meres affirmed.

"My goodness, you both sound so resolute, I'm getting all excited myself, have you any thoughts about it"? Shadrach asked.

"I don't think either of us have given much thought to the meaning, we both decided from the moment we saw it, you must be told immediately" answered Kedar.

"The observation platform has been set up with all we need, in half hour I hope to be looking at it myself" Shadrach paused for a moment before adding,

"If it is still there".

His old eyes twinkled as he grinned at his old students.

"We have seen it every night since" they both replied.

In that part of the world, you can watch the sun move below the horizon. Buildings, trees, hills, anything that the sun is shining on as it slowly sinks out of sight, seem to be transformed by a kaleidoscope of colours until it has gone completely below the sky.

Within minutes it is completely dark.

With eager anticipation Shadrach climbed the steps following Kedar and Meres, although he was much older he was still sprightly.

"Look at Regulas" Kedar instructed Shadrach.

Immediately his Mentor knew just where to begin observing.

Almost seconds later Shadrach replied, "I've got it".

"Now study the small stars above it".

Kedar waited in expectation for the reply.

"Well would you believe that, three extra little stars, just bright enough to be seen".

Meres and Kedar knew by the tone of his voice that he was as excited as they were.

Meres asked "What are your thoughts My Lord King".

Shadrach looked at his prodigies for a few moments without speaking, when he did finally reply, they had never known him so serious.

He said very quietly,

"Oh my young Princes, I'm so, so pleased you came to tell me, I feel that you are very privileged to have found these new little stars".

He took them both by the hand and added,

"This could be the sign the Jews have been waiting for, the Messiah could be on his way".

They stood for a few moments gripping each other by the hand.

Kings of the Yemen and many other groups who were not Hebrews had professed the Jewish faith for well over a hundred years.

"When did you first discover the stars Kedar"? asked Shadrach.

"Six nights ago", was the reply.

"And are they exactly as they were since then"? prompted Shadrach.

Kedar thought for a moment then asked,

"What do you think Meres?, I thought they may be a fraction lower".

"I agree" was the reply "they also seem a little brighter, or is it my imagination"?

"Yes I think you are right, I also thought the cluster seemed a little closer together" added Meres.

"You really think it may be the Messiah the Jews are waiting for, my Lord King"?

"I pick up from both of you that there is something special about the whole situation, you both have that feeling don't you"?

Shadrach sounded very sombre now.

"From that very moment of seeing the new stars I have had a wonderful tingling that I can not explain", replied Kedar.

"I also have a peculiar feeling, I can't explain it but it's somehow mysteriously wonderful" explained Meres.

"As soon as you arrived and told me you had found something in the stars, I also felt oddly moved", admitted Shadrach.

They continued to observe the new find for an hour, checking and comparing all relevant charts, finding older charts in case there was anything similar they could compare with, but nothing further came to light.

Suddenly a loud voice came from ground level below.

"So when I'm not around you have these secret meetings studying the stars".

The stargazers looked at each other in the moonlight, grinned and almost together they cried out,

"ASHPENAZ"!

Another member of the Student Princes had come to visit his uncle.

On arrival he had been told of the observation taking place and hurried along to join them.

"He's found his favorite uncle again" remarked Shadrach as he held out his arms to greet Ashpenaz.

"How did you know we were studying something wonderful"?

"Oh, if that's the case I'm really pleased I arrived back in time".

Ashpenaz had attended the convention and afterwards had family business to attend to in Kish.

He had made a stopover at Eshnunna not far away and decided to press on to arrive late.

"Someone has found a new star, I can feel it in my bones"

Ashpenaz looked at them quizzically and added,

"Come on, don't keep me in suspense".

"Let him look through the dioptra" said the King.

Before another word could be spoken Ashpenaz had jumped up to the side of Kedar and was looking at the stars where the instrument was in focus.

No one spoke, they were anxious to see how long it would take him to see anything unusual.

A minute or two went by then very slowly and quietly he said,

"Wow, who found them ? I guess it must be either Kedar or Meres, that's why you're both here".

"Always the analytical one" replied Uncle Shadrach,

"So you have seen the new cluster".

"Just above Leo, three making a triangle" affirmed Ashpenaz excitedly and continued, "You have not told me who discovered them yet".

"Six nights ago we were observing at Babylon and Kedar found them" Meres stated,

"We immediately thought of coming to tell King Shadrach".

"I feel very privileged and honored, I'm so glad you came to me first" replied Shadrach, he looked from one to the other before adding,

"You have made me so happy" there was a hint of a tear in his aged eyes.

Kedar had said very little but now ventured,

"King Shadrach has suggested it may be heralding the Jewish Messiah".

Now Ashpenaz adopted that very serious look, he turned to his uncle,

"Of course, my mind was on the find of a new star cluster that had always been there, but this could be altogether a new cluster, like comets and shooting stars".

"It must be observed continually to determine whether it follows its close neighbors or changes direction" Shadrach's voice now sounded very serious,

"The Jews have been waiting a very long time for a Great Leader, apparently it is forecast in their Holy Scriptures".

The four friends stood looking up at the stars, silent and deep in thought.

Suddenly Ashpenaz suggested,

"If it's to do with the Scriptures, we must go and see Jo".

Jo was short for Joiada, he was the fourth member of the student group that had formed a bond of friendship at the Alexandrian Academy so many years ago.

Joiada was also a Merchant Prince from Samaria, his family belonged to the Jews that were frowned upon by most of the other Jewish sects living in other parts of the world.

Joiada had been at the Nippur Convention and Meres suddenly remembered what he said,

"He's was going to Hit, his son is going to be Manager of a new Caravansary his family have built".

This was the latest in a chain of Caravansaries owned by Joiada's family.

"If he's stopping at Hit we could be there in a few days" proffered Kedar.

"I wish I was younger, I would have jumped at the chance to come along with you, my old bones are not taken to travelling long journeys. Something seems to tell me that you are going on a very long journey".

Now there was a hint of sadness in Shadrach's voice.

"You two are not going without me" exclaimed Ashpenaz.

"If the three of us turn up on Jo's doorstep he'll wonder what's hit him" laughed Meres.

Kedar chuckled,

"Just like old times, but he will know more about The Messiah, there is also another very important reason".

The other three looked at him quizzically in the moonlight.

"What more is there my young Prince"? Shadrach asked.

Kedar answered with a twinkle,

"The Star Cluster is going in that direction".

One hour before dawn their camels were ready and waiting with the necessary supplies for a few days Journey.

Their servants and bodyguards together made a party of nine men, with two pack camels totalling eleven in all.

King Shadrach was there to wish them a safe Journey but they could see that he was disappointed not being able to go with them.

"I shall watch that Cluster every night and track its Journey through the heavens until it goes down below the western horizon" he said resolutely.

"I estimate that from here you could track for seven months or so" Kedar said.

He had worked it out from the star group in which it was situated.

"There's no telling what you may witness from such a venture you about to undertake, may God be with you and keep you all safe".

Shadrach held up his arm to bless them, after bowing he turned and slowly walked back inside his palace.

The Caravan set off led by one of the guards, the three Princes rode in a group near the middle with a guard bringing up the rear, this was the formation almost the whole of the time they were to travel.

Since leaving the Convention at Nippur they could travel on the main Trade Route of the day, it was a very busy highway with lots of traffic going both ways.

This same highway followed between the two Great Rivers, it had been used for thousands of years.

These routes had brought riches to all the countries they passed through. They were so important that Darius, one of the Great Kings had built what became known as 'The Royal Route', from Susa in the south, to Sardis 1500 miles north east, in what is now Turkey.

Joiada and the New Caravansary

In the ancient city of HIT

Brightest and best of the sons of the morning,
Dawn on our darkness, and lend us thine aid.
(R Heber)

Three days later they covered the last few miles late in the day and arrived at dusk at the brand new Caravansary on the outskirts of the old City of Hit.

Although Hit had been a great City in it's day, it was now a much smaller community, Nomads came and went according to their whims or mainly moved to look for new pastures, according to their flocks.

A few farmers had built around the old city, making use of the fertile land.

Joiada's family had planned and built this latest new Caravan Station here to add to the facilities of the many travellers using this route.

Eli recognised the Royal Princes as they entered through the large winged shaped aperture leading into the quadrangle.

These entrances were so built to allow pack-camels to enter without being unloaded.

Most of these establishments were geared to take in whole caravan trains, which could deal with the needs of men, animals and all the various types of goods they carried.

Shaded cloisters surrounded the large rectangular yard, a few palm trees with a gravity fed fountain to grace the centre was just what was needed for men and animals to break their long Journey and enjoy such luxury.

This was the general pattern of these great purpose-built establishments.

They offered everything to the weary traveller.

An Inn, rented warehouse space, exchange or purchase of horse, camel or donkey.

A smallholding farm on the outside could supply most of the fresh food needed, with a generous supply of fresh water from the nearby river.

Local roadside markets (suks) were close by, this also helped to give the local peasants a living.

Eli sent immediately for his father Joiada and gave orders to his staff to attend to the Royal visitors and their entourage.

Within minutes Joiada's voice rang out around the complex.

He waited as they rode up to the reception area.

"Just because I told you of our new project I didn't think you would come to visit so soon".

A beaming smile shone out of a rugged, full bearded face of a tall broad shouldered man as he looked from one to the other.

Ashpenaz replied with a grin,

"We wanted to be among the first to try out the hospitality, if it doesn't meet our standard you could be blacklisted".

"Knowing you three there's a much more important reason for your most welcome visit" exclaimed Joiada, then added,

"How wonderful to see my brother Magi again so soon, please come and make yourselves at home".

They greeted each other like long lost comrades although it was only three weeks since they had attended the convention.

Over the many years the four Princes had kept in contact, their friendship had deepened as the years went by.

Joiada dealt with any pressing business and asked Eli to arrange the evening meal and make sure he was not disturbed as he entertained his distinguished guests.

He led them into a large well-furnished room which was all part of the Inn.

This room was reserved for family and important dignitaries.

Joiada stood as they entered and gave a small bow, the three guests greeted him with the same respect.

Protocol over they hugged each like long lost brothers.

The new servant staff waiting to serve them were somewhat amused and taken aback as they observed what they considered very unlike behaviour for such Royal Personnel.

Joiada noticed the effect it had on his staff. He and his friends were so amused they began to laugh.

"We promise to behave ourselves and not do anything we used to do when we were students so very long ago".

Ashpenaz assured them with a gesture of his hand.

This further amused the staff putting them at ease, especially some new young girls who were waiting in anticipation to serve them drinks.

After a very satisfying meal the Royal four reclined comfortably to sample the finest of wines and reminisce about the old days.

At least that was what Joiada thought they were to talk about.

He had no idea of the real reason for their visit until Meres spoke.

"We have something very important to show you later Joiada, and we need your expertise on a subject you understand far more than we do".

The serious look that came over their Royal host was so comical that the other three began to chuckle.

"Oh if you can grin about it I need not worry, I thought for a moment it might be something serious".

Joiada sounded relieved.

Ashpenaz followed with,

"It could be the most important happening of your life".

Again that very serious look appeared as Joiada stared from one to the other.

Kedar almost shouted,

"Let's tell him all about or he will burst".

"I had an idea it must be something very special to have brought the three of you all this way to visit me", Joiada exclaimed with a sigh of relief.

"After the Convention ended and we went our separate ways, Kedar and myself decided to go to the old observatory at Babylon for a stargazing session".

Meres decided to start right from the beginning.

He continued, "Kedar has found a new Star Cluster".

Joiada looked very surprised, this was the very last thing he would have expected.

"Never", was Joiada's first emphatic reply, but the staid look on their faces told him it must be true.

Seconds later he shouted one of the servants and told him to fetch Eli immediately.

Ashpenaz asked hopefully,

"Are we going star gazing"?

"We certainly are, I want to see for myself this find that is so important to bring you such a distance in order to tell me about it"

Joiada's voice betrayed his excitement.

An hour later it was almost dusk, Eli had the large wooden platform organised with the apparatus needed for their surveillance.

Although it was a wooden structure it had been purpose built inside and affixed to the perimeter wall of the compound.

A wooden stairway led up to the platform that was large enough to accommodate the four of them.

As soon as they ascended Kedar set his dioptra to observe his new found Cluster.

Although there was no moon that night the stars themselves seemed to have a welcome glow they had not noticed before.

As soon as the stars began to appear Kedar was ready in minutes and moved aside from the instrument for Joiada to look through, he gave a clue to the position.

"There they are, three small stars but they seem to want to talk to us, they are in a line between Regulas and Algeba".

Joiada moved to Kedar's dioptra, he now knew exactly what to look for.

A moment later he exclaimed,

"That's a proper little triangle isn't it".

Meres and Ashpenaz were also fixed on the new Cluster, Aspenaz affirmed,

"They do seem brighter Kedar".

Meres agreed and asked,

"What do you think Joiada"?

"I'm thinking that you want my advice about the significance of the Cluster".

Then took them totally by surprise by adding,

"You are wondering about the Messiah we are expecting aren't you"?

His three Royal Visitors were astonished by his answer.

"Uncle Shadrach's first thoughts after seeing the Cluster were about your Messiah", replied Meres.

"The Messiah will be for all mankind everywhere, my friends it will be your Messiah if you wish to follow Him".

Then he followed with "I hope you will".

They were studying for almost an hour before descending the platform and moving back into the complex.

After enjoying a sumptuous meal they were led into a smaller more intimate room.

Comfortably sipping choice wines their thoughts were crammed with questions to ask.

Joiada had excused himself while he went to fetch his Scriptures.

He soon came bustling into the cosy room with a wooden box full of scrolls of papyrus. Some of them looked quite old but one set was outstandingly new.

It was the new bundle that he took out and placed on his lap as he sat and addressed his friends.

"I'm so excited I feel all fingers and thumbs, I've been searching through a chest that I try to have at my disposal whenever I have time to spare, I keep telling myself that my sons are quite capable to run the business without me but I can't help wanting to take part personally".

"We understand how you must feel, your family reputation is highly regarded along many of the Trade Routes and the Great

Rivers, all the way down to Egypt, said Ashpenaz and followed with,

"Uncle Shadrach is always singing your praises Joiada".

Joiada looked across at Ashpenaz who belonged to one of the richest families in that part of the world, he was rather taken aback, then replied.

"That's very kind of King Shadrach, it is good that our families have such trust and confidence in each other, if only all men shared that same brotherhood together".

The three Royal visitors were all eager to know what the Scriptures would reveal.

Meres was prompted to ask,

"Does anything come to mind before you start searching"?

"My old father, God Bless him, has a favourite quote, I can hear him saying it now" answered Joiada,

"It is from one of the lesser known prophets named Zechariah"

Kedar couldn't wait any longer,

"Come on Joiada, tell us what it is".

Without thinking Joiada went on about being a young Jewish boy albeit classed as lesser Jews.

He went on to explain,

"All Jewish boys are taught by rote as soon as they can remember things, the strict Jews have sayings or quotations from the scriptures written on small parchments to carry in the little container fastened round their head".

"That's called a phylactery isn't it"? exclaimed Ashpenaz.

"Yes that's right, so you know how important we regard the Scriptures, we are not so stringent in our way of serving God, but having said that we do follow in our own way".

"Tell us what your father used to say" Meres almost shouted".

"It was Almighty God Himself telling Zechariah,

'Shout and be glad, O daughter of Zion,
for I am coming and I will live among you'.
Many nations will be joined with the Lord
In that day and will become My people. Zech 2,10-11

No one spoke for what seemed hours.

Ashpenaz was the first to break the silence. He spoke very quietly and slowly as he asked,

"God Himself said that"?

"When Prophets received instructions by visions, dreams, or by actually hearing God Himself, he either had to tell what God wanted the people to do or what God Himself had actually said.

This was one that God said, HE HIMSELF, was going to do".

Joiada looked at his friends, he saw very plainly his answer had had a profound effect on them.

Kedar and Meres repeated one after the other,

"God Himself".

"If that is not telling us that Someone very Great is coming, I don't know what is",Joiada reiterated.

This information brought a much more serious side to the conversation.

Ashpenaz gave a long low,

"OOH" and followed with,

"And that is your dad's favourite saying".

"We would often be having a discussion in the family, perhaps during meal times and he would put his hand in the air and suddenly shout,

'God is coming to live with us',

We became so used to it we would make some bland reply and then all carry on as though the remark was part of the discourse".

Kedar reminded them what had prompted the Prophecy,

"Do you believe the new Cluster could be pointing to your father's favourite quote".

Joiada thought long and hard before replying,

"If the new Cluster is so obvious to us it would have been charted, I feel it must be something brand new, Astronomers regard all new stars as signs that bring tidings of a great happening. Some prophecies of The Messiah were predicted seven hundred years ago. What else could it mean"?

"What do you propose we do Joiada"?

Meres sounded so excited.

"If you think the position of the cluster is going to remain fairly constant we could work out how long it will be before it goes down in the west".

Then Joiada really surprised them by adding,

"I would be willing to follow it to see what might be revealed".

This statement really astounded them.

They had believed it was something very extraordinary from the very first sighting but it had now gone beyond anything they could have dreamed of.

Kedar's brow showed deep furrows, eventually he asked,

"You are willing to follow, it could be a long, long journey".

"I have a strong feeling that it will be worth every minute of every mile" was the reply.

Again the three friends were stunned. They had not expected this reaction from Joiada, never dreaming that he would be so moved about the star sign.

"If you wish to follow, I'm coming with you" Kedar exclaimed.

"You can make that three" added Meres.

"What makes you think you can go without me"? Ashpenaz exclaimed.

Joiada's face slowly lit up with his lovable smile.

He looked from one to the other and addressed them like an elder brother as he said,

"My great comrades of old, you have made me so happy, it looks as though our Messiah has called us to follow Him".

The next few days were spent working out how long it would be before the new cluster would be falling out of sight.

This is the Astronomers term for stars going down in the western sky as opposed to rising in the east.

They estimated that it 'rose' with the known stars some time in Sivian, (May) and would 'fall' sometime around Kislev. (middle of December)

This would take over eight months from rising to falling.

Their journey would take them westward but how far, they did not know.

Travelling west from Hit meant that they could at least for the time being still follow the Trade Route.

Joiada's family had Caravansaries at Dura-Europos, Palmyra and Damascus, all of which were along the westward route.

They would change their direction only if the Cluster did not keep to its path with the surrounding stars.

Planning such a journey was all part and parcel to Joiada and his staff, they did it day in and day out, so within a couple of days it was all organised.

By using the 'great highways' of the day, they could quite easily follow or if they wished, travel in front of the Cluster and wait for it to catch up.

Once Joiada had told Eli what was required he spent time studying the Scriptures. Later the following day they were gathered after the mid-day meal in the same room as before, Joiada was eager to enlighten them further with his latest readings.

He began by telling them about his new copies of the Scriptures.

"When our forefathers were taken into Exile by Nebuchadnezzar most of our Scriptures had either been lost or destroyed.

One of the most learned Jews named Ezra decided he must try to collect all the copies he could and write down what the elders could relate from being taught by rote".

Ezra was a scribe, like our lawyer, it was second nature for him to work on such a project.

"How long ago was that exactly"? asked Meres.

"Five hundred and twenty years ago. Ezra collected as much as he could and we are thankful to him, but my family and many other Samaritans are not pleased with some other decisions Ezra agreed to".

Joiada's voice had changed suddenly, he now sounded quite upset.

"You sound very angry now Joiada, what was that about"? Ashpenaz asked.

Joiada looked down before he replied, he was truly hurt at the thoughts of having to tell them about the following incident, especially after saying how good Ezra was.

Joiada continued, "He and another leading Jew, Nehemiah,

organised the Jewish Exiles into returning to Judea and Jerusalem and they did a very good job of it. It must have been a very big undertaking, but what many of the Jews had done while living in Babylon was mingle with people of other races. Human nature being what it is many Jews had taken foreign wives".

Ashpenaz chuckled and said,

"I wouldn't have expected anything else".

Joiada enlightened further,

"The Jewish people were chosen to be different.

From the very beginning Abraham was told only to choose wives from his brothers family, only after hundreds of years would they have greater choice of choosing their partners, Abraham himself married his half sister Sarah".

"That was very close breeding, what did Ezra do to upset your ancestors", Meres asked.

But he almost guessed what the answer was going to be.

"He told the men with foreign wives they must divorce them and send them away including any children they had" replied Joiada.

Now they realised and could see how hurt Joiada was.

With what Joiada said next only added to his distress.

He proceeded to tell them what happened to his ancestor recorded in Nehemiah 13, 28.

"Many of them like my family refused and went to live in Samaria, the people there were very mixed.

Nebuchadnezzar had relocated many of his prisoners there, it was also the old Kingdom of Israel, the Jews who had remained there had continued their way of life as best they could, worshipping the God of Abraham. Naturally my ancestors along with the other ostracised Jews settled down with them.

Over the years we have become our own nation proving ourselves among the best Merchants worldwide".

This brought a very different mood to the proceedings that had begun as a joyous get-together.

"According to Uncle Shadrach your Family Name is one of the most respected across the whole of the land" affirmed Ashpenaz.

Joiada looked at him assuredly and gave a little smile.

"Thank you Ashpenaz, King Shadrach is not biased like the strict Jews, I know some of them who would like to treat us like dirt", came the reply.

Meres asked tentatively,

"Excuse me Joiada, but is that the reason why you say the Jerusalem Jews are so high and mighty"?

"You said it Meres, that is just what it's all about, they regard all Samaritans as lower class, especially the Pharisees, but over the years we have proved we are as good as them", replied Joiada emphatically.

"There are Jews in every country and like people everywhere there are good and bad, whether they are from Jerusalem or anywhere in Judea" remarked Kedar.

Suddenly Joiada changed the subject altogether by asking,

"Have you given the new Star Cluster a name"?

Kedar blinked and humbly replied,

"We're not going to call it Kedar".

"Why not" Ashpenaz exclaimed, "You found it".

Meres agreed, "Yes Kedar, you should have the honour, what say you Joiada"?

Joiada went deep in thought again for a moment and said,

"You came to ask my advice of what it may mean, I think you should have the honour".

"There are three stars making a triangle, how about calling it Triune"? Kedar suggested quietly.

The others thought for a moment, Joiada answered,

"That is a very apt name.

Your name will be recorded as the discoverer of Triune".

"If that is your suggestion, that is what we will call it, do you agree Ashpenaz"? asked Meres.

"That is fine by me, it has a certain ring to it, Triune !", declared Ashpenaz.

Eli came and interrupted them to speak to Joiada. They had planned on looking at the stars again for an hour.

"I think you had better cancel the star study tonight father, a dust storm has suddenly come up from the east, I don't think you would see very much".

They each said how disappointed they were but star gazing would definitely be out of the question.

Sand storms disrupted everything outdoors, many things had to be covered, especially eyes, until the storm blew itself out.

"You could explain more about the Scriptures" prompted Kedar.

"Tell me when you've had enough" laughed Joiada

"I could go on all night".

"We'll tell you when your good wine begins to make us drowsy", added Ashpenaz.

The first thing Meres thought about from previous talks prompted him to say,

"If Ezra gathered the lost Scriptures together again, there wouldn't have been many copies about".

"That leads onto this new copy I bought the last time I was in Alexandria".

Joiada excitedly reached into his box and showed them the brand new set of papyrus sheets, bound in sections to make several books.

"I'm proud of these, they can now produce copies much quicker and cheaper".

The other princes could tell by his tone of voice how pleased he was with his latest copies.

"How do they do that"? inquired Meres.

"A group of educated slaves, perhaps twenty or so are seated at desks with materials for writing, they write it down as a tutor dictates it.

This method enables many copies to be written all at the same time, copies of the books gathered by Ptolemy Philadelphus can now be enjoyed by far more scholars and the price of each copy is much cheaper than when it was copied individually".

"I didn't think the Jewish Scriptures would have been allowed to be copied, they don't like sharing their scriptures do they"? queried Ashpenaz.

"Over two hundred years ago Philadelphus asked the Jerusalem

Jews to allow him to have a copy. Many of them did not agree, they wished to keep their Holy Writings to themselves" answered Joiada.

"Then how did he persuade them"? asked Kedar.

"After Alexander came many Jews chose the Greek way of life, it was much more freer than their strict code of living, much more appealing, they became 'Hellenists'".

"Did they just give copies to the library"? asked Ashpenaz.

"No, it was much more involved than that.

Seventy two elders, supposedly six from each of the twelve Jewish Tribes were invited to go to Alexandria. Each one dictated what they could remember by rote, together with what written copies they had. The result was quite a comprehensive compilation of the whole Word of God".

"Is that what you have there"? Kedar asked.

Joiada held up the set of Manuscripts it was obvious how proud he was with them.

"You haven't read all those since you bought them have you"? Meres asked.

"No I haven't had time, what I want to read is the set of the Book of Prophets, and that is quite enough for the time being" Joiada replied.

"I think we should retire and leave you to do a bit of studying" said Ashpenaz.

"I don't want to miss our company together, I'm so enjoying your presence, but it would be helpful if you don't mind" pleaded Joiada.

While Joiada studied his new set of scriptures, his three friends moved to another room. Outside there were still some light dust clouds in the air, not suitable for looking through instruments to study stars.

They decided to retire early.

The following morning it was a hive of activity.

Most of the staff were outside sweeping the sand away and making the complex spick and span.

Joiada and his family liked to present their new compound clean and tidy.

However, Meres, Kedar and Ashpenaz were up an hour before dawn and were able to see the new Triune they had named.

"It seems slightly brighter each time I see it" Kedar commented.

"And it has moved slightly lower don't you think"? asked Meres.

"I agree with that" replied Ashpenaz.

"It is very slightly, but if it continues to get brighter over the period of months, there's no telling how bright it will be when it goes down" said Kedar eagerly.

They heard a scuffle as they spoke, Joiada was climbing the steps to join them just as the first glimpse of light appeared in the east but Joiada was able to have a few minutes to look at Triune before the sun put all the stars out one by one.

"I am so pleased you came" exclaimed Joiada as they were packing their instruments away then he spoke to Kedar,

"I'm also thrilled to bits with the dioptra you made Kedar.

"Well I didn't make yours particularly, but everyone I know who has one seems very pleased with them" answered Kedar.

His three friends agreed so much so that Kedar was a little embarrassed.

The dioptras they now used had been made by Kedar's family company, and presented to them as gifts.

Kedar and his new team of engineers had improved the earlier models making them more accurate for recording and plotting the stars. His ancestors were Arameans from near Allepo.

Four generations previously, the family became involved in the metal industry, iron and copper were mined not far from their home, they developed new ways of smelting alloys, mixing tin and copper to make brass and bronze.

Later, when Greece became over populated, some of them emigrated to the lands they conquered bringing new skills of engineering, some came to live near Kedar's home.

Two of them had worked with the men who had invented the first analogue computer designed by Greek Astronomers to workout the distances and positions of the sun, moon and planets at a given date.

The machine worked by turning a cog wheel with a hand crank, which in turn moved a set of about thirty gears.

The gearing was able to produce the astronomical information required.

It is believed to have been invented sometime between 200 and 100 BC, but unfortunately, while It was being transported by ship it sank off the Greek Island of Antikythera, it was retrieved by sponge divers in 1900, it is now kept in the museum at Athens.

The two Greek engineers that came to live near Kedar's ancestors were so taken with the quality of the alloys produced at the smelting works, they began to design and make all kinds of instruments for navigation, astronomy, measuring and plotting time and distances.

These instruments became sort after by all the leading surveyors, geographers and astronomers throughout the known world.

The Family Business also had dealings with the Great Jewish Banking and Shipping house of Saramalla in Antioch who's wealth and munificence had provided the gold and silver that would cover the new Gates leading to the New Temple being built by Herod.

"The new dioptras have certainly been quite a boon following Triune" said Meres.

"I'm so pleased with mine, it is much more accurate than previous ones I have used", added Ashpenaz,

"I can't wait to see the new position each time I use it".

Although the stars had disappeared in the morning sunlight the four Royal Princes continued looking up into the sky for a few minutes until Joiada spoke.

"Come on let's go plan the next stage of the journey".

The rest of that day was spent sorting the provisions and animals needed for a long expedition.

The direction would still be westwards, but as yet, they did not know where.

With their bodyguards and attendants this made a company of twelve men. Each riding a camel with three pack camels, they also took three pack asses.

They would not be travelling as a Caravan Train, with most of their animals having it's own rider to lead it, they could move much faster.

In a Train of camels a 'Caravan Puller' is needed while each camel is tied to the one in front. The Puller rides a donkey pulling a rope attached to a peg in the nose of the leading camel, one puller for every ten camels. Many Camel Pullers or 'Leaders' became politicians. They were called Syndiachs, some became so famous they achieved Political Power.

Mohamed was a Camel Puller. Some busts of famous 'Pullers', can still be seen in museums around the Middle East.

All the provisions and animals would be ready for an early start the following morning.

After the evening meal, there was a buzz of excitement as they sat together in the cosy room as before.

"Have you found anything in the Scriptures Joiada"? asked Ashpenaz.

"I haven't come across where or which way to go, for the time being we will follow the Trade Route west. If I keep having a read I'm sure I shall find a clue" answered Joiada.

"Did you find *anything* alluding to the Messiah"? Meres inquired.

"We were always told that the Prophet Isaiah was the most prolific writer about The Messiah, so that is where I have begun. Last night when you left me I found something that many people will challenge".

This brought very puzzled looks to all their faces now.

Kedar's brow furrowed as he asked, "What makes you say that Joiada"?

He looked at them quizzically, then quoted,

"A Virgin shall conceive and bear a Son,
and He will be called Emmanuelle, God with us". Isa 7,14.

"Those Scriptures are certainly full of surprises", Meres exclaimed.

"I see what you mean by being challenged",
followed Ashpenaz.

"I've got to admit it has puzzled me very much" admitted Joiada.

Kedar suddenly interrupted,

"Yes but most of the dessert people now follow the God of Abraham. It's because of the way he has led you and provided for you. We also wish to be a branch under His protection to look after us also. Surely, if God is so great, He could quite easily create a Special Child from a Virgin".

They all stared at Kedar, then a look of enlightenment showed on Joiada's face as he added,

"What a brilliant answer, nothing is impossible to God".

"Especially when He tells us way in advance what is going to happen", said Meres.

"Remind me again, when did you first see Triune" asked Joiada.

"We arrived at Babylon about the end of Sivian, (May) its now near the end of Tammuz, (June) just about one month ago", replied Meres.

"If we head towards Dura-Europos where we have another Caravan Station it will be about two months when Triune arrives there", stated Joiada.

"That's about one hundred and fifty miles, again we will be able to get in front of Triune and wait there observing it's approach" Meres added.

"That is good thinking Meres, everything is ready for an early start tomorrow" replied Joiada.

"Have you given a thought to gifts"? asked Ashpenaz.

This changed the subject altogether.

Ashpenaz had thought once or twice, but now he had mentioned it, they all realised the significance and the protocol involved.

The Messiah would be *The* most important *Deity* on earth.

This suddenly made them become conscious of just how important this Holy Person was.

"With you arriving out of the blue like you did, then seeing Triune, and you asking about our Messiah's expectation, I never gave a thought to gifts, Ashpenaz you have reminded us of something most essential"

"Does Isaiah give us any clue regarding His status"? Kedar asked.

"Very much so" answered Joiada, "I was going to mention it before retiring but talking about what gifts to take with us should be sorted now".

As Joiada finished talking he was reaching for his Book of Prophets.

After finding the place he recited,

"For unto us a Child is born, unto us a Son is given
And the government will be upon His shoulders.
And He will be called Wonderful, Counsellor,
Mighty God, everlasting Father, Prince of Peace". Isa 9,6

Five minutes passed by.
Each on of them deep in thought.
It seemed almost hours before Meres spoke quietly,
"How can we find gifts for such a Holy Person, He will be The Son of God"?

Another short silence before Kedar asked,
"Do you think we are worthy to embark on this mission Joiada"?

"I feel that we must pursue our journey and leave it in God's Hands, if it is not to be, it won't be" answered Joiada.

"Well spoken Joiada, I am positive about going whatever the outcome" said Ashpenaz.

The sentiment between them now had increased all the more, each one of them felt compelled to complete this assignment at all costs.

"Now we *can* sought out some gifts" exclaimed Ashpenaz.

"Gold for a King" shouted Kedar.

"For such a Holy King, we must take frankincense" added Joiada.

"If The Messiah is to be born of a Virgin as Isaiah says, He will also be The Son of Man" Meres reminded them.

"All Holy Men are anointed, usually with Myrrh" added Joiada,

"Moses was given a recipe for mrryh by our Lord God Himself". (Exodus 30, 22-25)

"Then we must include Myrrh" Kedar concluded.

"That's settled then, Gold, Frankincense and Myrrh",

Kedar shouted.

"I have just the very thing" remarked Joiada, "As they were building this complex the workmen unearthed a metal box of gold darics".

"A box full, how big was the box"? asked Ashpenaz with his usual grin.

"They must have been honest workmen" exclaimed Meres.

Joiada laughed at Meres' remark,

"As it happened, Eli was with them.

He gave each one of them a few coins and they were satisfied".

Ashpenaz reminded him of his question,

"And was it a large box"?

"It contained nearly two thousand" answered Joiada also with a big grin on his face.

Kedar commented "I suppose someone had buried it when they heard about one of the invaders coming to take over".

"Apparently it could have been Alexander" Joiada informed them.

"Were you told that by the locals"? asked Kedar.

"There was a story among them that when Alexander reached Susa, near the old Palace he found a large cache of gold ingots, including bags of gold darics. It is believed the coins had been collected as tax over the many years", Joiada informed them.

"Golden coins collected in tax and melted down". Ashpenaz nearly choked as he thought of how many coins were entailed in the operation.

"You think your coins would be part of that collection"? asked Meres.

"After hearing other stories from the tribesmen around, one or two more boxes and leather bags of coins have been found between here and Susa, so it may well all be part of that collection, probably it was dumped when they knew the Greeks were coming" added Joiada.

"Alexander would be highly delighted with it however large the hoard" Kedar said.

"According to the locals, it was a very large amount" Joiada laughed as he saw the look on their faces.

Gold darics were minted by Darius II, King of Persia, they were quite thin and only 15mm in diameter, it made them wonder how many years the taxes had been accumulated.

Joiada explained why he had told them of the find.

"I'm sure gold coins would be a useful gift to present to a new born babe, who according to the Prophet, would be the King of Kings"

"You will be willing to do that"? Kedar asked.

"They would have been taken from ordinary people over many years, it would be fitting to present them to The Messiah".

"Any gift given will only be a token, it will show that we pay homage to our Creator", added Meres.

"It will not be a problem getting Frankincense and Myrrh on this Trade Route, Ashpenaz remarked, "Will it"?

As he spoke he looked directly at Meres.

Joiada and Kedar also turned and looked at Meres.

Meres began to smile as he stared back at his friends, he paused and then replied rather sheepishly.

"Of course it wont be a problem, I'll send word directly, where do you think I should have it delivered"?

Meres's family had become one of the biggest producers of Myrrh, they exported it to the four corners of the known world.

One of his ancestors had been among the seven Wise Men, who were courtiers of King Axerxes of Persia during the Exile.

The book of Esther tells of women in the Kings harem having twelve months beauty treatment before being chosen by the King. (Est 1,14 and 2, 12)

This particular ancestor of Meres had built an Estate near Asshur on the south bank of the River Tigris.

Near the area where they settled was boggy ground where clumps of irises grew. This species of the flag family produced Calamus, an ingredient used to mix with oils and balms and sought after by the beauticians that attended the ladies of the harem.

In this same area grew trees of which the bark produced Sweet Cinnamon.

Eventually the family had the idea of obtaining and growing whatever other plants could be used for mixing and making not only oils and balms for the Beauty industry but also for Medical use.

Now the family industry had become one of the leading suppliers of these products throughout the world.

Trees and plants of all kinds had been planted that produced Cassia, Stacte, Galbanum, Onycha and Flowering Myrrh.

What was not grown on the Estate, they traded with countries that could supply their needs.

"How much should we take" asked Meres.

They discussed it among themselves, Joiada said,

"The myrrh will be in a bottle or cask".

After more discussion Meres gave his point of view.

"How about two logs of myrrh and one mina of Frankincense"?

(2 logs= 1 pint----1 mina= over one pound in weight)

"I think that amount of each will make fitting gifts" replied Kedar.

"If we stay at our Caravansaries the last one on route will be Damascus, have them delivered there Meres" said Joiada.

"Great" Ashpenaz declared, "What wonderful gifts for a most Divine Person".

It was now half an hour after dusk and they wanted to look at Triune before retiring for the night.

Eli called his father to report their equipment had been prepared for them.

Joiada spoke first after they had begun their observations.

"Kedar, to think that you noticed such a small Cluster out of all the stars in the sky, I'm sure *you were the one,* destined to find it".

"Do you realise how important that makes you"? Meres exclaimed.

"Don't tell him that Meres, he will be wanting to pull rank" laughed Ashpenaz.

"I mentioned it because we could be the only ones in the whole world, following its course", Joiada reminded them.

Kedar had just been listening, but by the lantern light he was busy with his dividers, after taking a reading he remarked,

"I'm sure that since we first plotted it, it has moved slightly southwest".

They all took readings, after checking and double checking, Meres replied,

"Yes, very little each night since our observations began but its quite noticeable now with a slight change of position to the other stars".

The quest to follow the Star-cluster became such a great craving, the four Princes went about their tasks of preparation almost without realising how it had taken over their lives.

The following morning by the third hour (9-0am) found them once again well on their way along what was known as the 'Royal Road' built by King Darius.

Three hours later they came to a shady place close to the river.

The Princes decided to rest during the hottest part of the day.

Their attendants would have dealt with all the animals but the Princes always settled their own mounts themselves.

When all had been fed and watered two of the servants went off to get some fresh fruit from one of the local 'suks'.

"I wonder where our mission will take us"?
mused Ashpenaz.

They had made themselves comfortable half sitting, half lying on the various bundles that the camels carried.

"How many returned to Jerusalem with Ezra"? asked Meres, he sat next to Joiada as he questioned him.

After thinking about it Joiada replied,

"They left in groups, the first batch over seven hundred years ago, then another group twenty years later. The Judean Jews did not return until over one hundred years later. When they could return, all the ones from Judea wanted to live in Jerusalem but because of their great numbers that was impossible".

After a pause he added,

"There were far too many of them to live in the City itself, the others had to take residence in other parts of Judea" he continued.

"How did they choose where they could live"? Ashpenaz inquired.

"Lots were taken, one family in ten to live in Jerusalem, the others had to live elsewhere" Joiada informed them.

"The Jewish Community that were left to live between the rivers is much bigger that those in Judea, isn't it"? Kedar exclaimed and continued, "Far more must have decided to stay in Babylonia than the ones returning".

"You're quite right there Kedar, in the seventy years during the Exile, many of them had built up businesses too good to leave, not only that, many were working for the government, they were even trusted to keep state secrets, obviously the Babylonians did not want them to leave".

A light meal was served as Joiada enlightened them more of his Jewish history.

He continued, "Strabo the famous Rabbi in Jerusalem quoted, 'there is not a land that does not have Jews living there', the Jewish Community between the rivers are not only the largest of all Jewish Settlements they are also the wealthiest."

"How do the others get on with them" asked Ashpenaz.

Joiada chuckled before replying,

"Between the two communities it is, us and them.

The Babylonian Jews still speak mostly Hebrew, the Judeans and Egyptian Jews now mostly speak Greek".

"And your people, the Samaritans, are classed different to either of them"? asked Kedar.

"Oh yes, we are nowhere near good enough for either of them, unless they wish to do business with us, then we are all equal" laughed Joiada.

"Jews are always willing to make transactions to make money with anyone" added Meres.

"Yes Meres, you know only too well, when poor Jews need to

go into the Temple at Jerusalem they are only allowed to pay their Temple Tax using Temple currency, so the money changers sit in the Temple Court getting rich from their own people by charging high exchange rates for them to pay the Temple Tax in the correct coinage".

"Don't the Authorities keep a check on such transactions"? Ashpenaz asked.

"The High Priests are very strict, like all Races, some are good, others will turn a blind eye", returned Joiada.

Kedar had been thinking about the different Jewish Sections and asked,

"You seem to be poles apart, how about The Messiah, do all Jewish settlements believe He will come"?

"We all follow the Scriptures in our own way, the Prophecy is there for us all to read, yes all Jews are expecting The Messiah" Joiada was quite adamant.

Meres' quiet voice asked,

"Are they all expecting a Prince of Peace"?

This made each of them wonder about what sort of Deity would come to this Race of People that God had fashioned by calling Abraham almost two thousand years ago.

Even Joiada was trying to be careful with his answer, he also had heard all sorts of expectations from the many scattered Jews he had been in contact with involving his family business.

"I've got to admit that I've not had chance to read Isaiah before, as I told you earlier, the Scriptures I owned were very fragmented, nothing like this new set of manuscripts. To tell you the truth I did not expect a Prophecy quite like that. A 'Prince of Peace' is nothing at all to what is expected".

Joiada answered somewhat with of a note of concern.

"Wouldn't it be a wonderful happening if we did have a 'Prince of Peace"? Kedar commented.

"I'm sure sometime over the last few years I've heard mention of a warrior Messiah" Ashpenaz added.

"Yes, no one has ever dreamed of a Great Leader to be a Prince of Peace, let us look forward to seeing the 'Prince of Peace", Joiada exclaimed hopefully.

They all nodded in agreement.

During the hottest part of the day they rested, temperatures were 37' c.

After sunset a westerly breeze made a refreshing change, the first thing was for their attendants to unpack just enough star gazing equipment for one of them to use and take turns for a quick check on the Triune Cluster.

Ashpenaz was the first to pick up the dioptra and focused up into the sky, minutes later he remarked,

"It must be brighter, I picked it out it quite easily tonight".

As each took a turn to view their discovery the more they were filled with awe.

"Each time I see it I think I must be dreaming" exclaimed Kedar.

"If it stays with Leo Minor we can easily continue well in front" Meres added.

Suddenly a group of horsemen were heard and went by at a gallop while they were gazing up.

The noise made their mounts restless as the servants were loading them to move on.

They had camped twenty yards off the well-worn path, and the whole group watched as the horses disappeared.

Two of the body-guards came running, one shouted,

"I'm sure they were just passing in a hurry my Lord Ashpenaze, we think it was a Roman Scout group".

"Thank you" replied Ashpenaz, "I'm sure you're right Rufus"

"Only a Squad then" Joiada said "let's hope we don't see any more".

A new moon gave fair light for them as they set off a few minutes later.

They followed in the wake of a caravan bound for Greece, but with moving at a faster pace they were soon overtaking them.

As they passed, greetings and pleasantries were exchanged with the other men who also agreed it must have been a Roman Squad that passed them earlier.

With such an amount of caravan traffic using these Routes, it gave travellers a certain assurance of safety. Caravan leaders were always more cautious if they were alone, or near wooded areas, or if their route lay between hills where bandits could lay in ambush.

Dura-Europos

Hail, the heaven born Prince of Peace! Hail, the Son of Righteousness!
`Light and life to all He brings, Risen with healing in His wings.
(C Wesley)

Five days later they approached the City of Dura-Europos.

The Seleucids built it as a Border City in 303 BC., on the right bank of the Euphrates.

A controlled River Crossing had been set up over a substantial bridge.

It was always in great demand for the traffic using the Trade Route.

Flat-bottomed boats large and small also plied up and down the river, as they had done so for 2000 years.

Many Riverside Cities had great wharves and well organised Police and Customs authorities to keep trade and travellers in order.

The Caravansary was two miles before the City itself, during the last few miles their pace had slowed considerably due to the volume of trading caravans.

For this last leg to Dura-Europos, they had set off an hour before dawn, it was now the forth hour (10 am.), the sun was already very hot.

A familiar voice greeted Joiada as he led them into yet another of the Family Complexes, this time by one of his nephews.

Simian was a tall handsome young man who was clearly delighted to see his uncle,

"What an honour for you to visit us Prince Joiada, I see you have brought Royal Visitors with you".

He and his staff bowed low as the entourage moved into the quadrangle.

Within minutes each member of the Royal Party and their attendants had a servant holding their mounts ready to administer to their needs.

Joiada did not wish to say too much about the Star Quest at the moment so he replied,

"Greetings Simion, my Royal friends and I are studying something special with the stars, it involves takings readings along this route so we may be here for a few nights".

"Please stay as long as you wish Uncle, we will be honoured to serve you and your guests".

The four Princes were made welcome in the shady cloisters where comfortable seating was arranged and a refreshing meal brought after they had bathed and changed.

Joiada had acquired his scriptures before settling down.

Meres was enjoying a slice of water melon.

After wiping his chin he said,

"We are very blessed to be able to enjoy such amenities, we are in debt to you and your family".

"I am so pleased that we can be of such service, but I'm sure we will not always be so fortunate along our Journey, there's no telling where Triune will finally end our quest" replied Joiada.

"Do you have any more prophecies for us"? asked Ashpenaz.

Joiada looked serious before answering,

"I was restless after settling down to sleep under the stars last night, I went to Seth and asked him to light a lantern for me, I had the urge to look at the manuscripts".

"I perceived you were studying something, but I soon dozed off, did you find anything"? Kedar asked.

"Still looking at Isaiah I read,

Nations shall come to your light
and Kings to the brightness of Your Dawn" Isa 60,3

Again after Joiada had read the prophecy, a sort of respectful silence descended upon them.

Meres was the first to speak and in his quiet voice he asked,

"Could we be so blessed to see the Messiah at the brightness of His Dawn"?

Meres' statement added further to the ambience, as they sat under the cloisters quite close to the busy life inside and outside the Caravansary.

A great many merchants were going about their business as the staff attended to their needs.

Yet the four close royals seemed to be alone on a planet of their own as they mulled over Isaiah's prophecy.

"To think it was written seven hundred years ago makes it all the more fascinating" exclaimed Ashpenaz.

"Have you come across a clue as to where it will be" asked Kedar.

Joiada shook his head,

"Not yet, I don't know where to look" he replied.

"Let's hope you will have some inspiration again, I'm sure that's what you had last night" commented Meres.

After their refreshments, as the sun rose to it's highest point in the heavens the heat brought most activities to a halt, and the four Princes drifted into a sleepy siesta.

Almost one hour after dusk a refreshing breeze from the east changed the conditions into a hive of activity. Lanterns lit the pathways, oil lamps shone out from the windows as the Merchants discussed with each other what their latest prices or exchange rates for goods on the market would be.

Senior Directors of Joiada's Family were there for sales or exchanges of any animal of burden used in the transport of their wares.

The four Princes had gone to the observation tower, it was situated away from any lights that may detract gazing up at the night sky.

Not even the wisp of a cloud was around as they each set up their own instruments for individual observations.

One of the recent new stars to rise was Spica in the Constellation of Virgo.

It was a very bright large star, southwest of the new Cluster of the three they had named Triune.

Kedar made the first comment.

"I'm sure it has moved further away from Leo Minor".

"Yes definitely" added Kedar, "towards Denebola".

Joiada had his sighting now and followed with,

"Another week or so and it could be level with Denebola".

Ashpenaz was also on sight now, "If it continues to follow that course it could get very close to Spica", he exclaimed.

"If that is so it will be much lower in the sky when it falls" added Joiada, "I hope we are able to fulfil what we set out to do".

"I have a feeling that we have been assigned to fulfil the undertaking of a lifetime" exclaimed Meres.

"The three stars are so much brighter, how can they be this bright since that first sighting"? asked Kedar.

No one spoke for a few minutes, all four were wrapped up with their studies of the night sky.

Then Joiada and Ashpenaz almost spoke together,

"Perhaps they will form a Conjunction with Spica".

They looked at each in the light of the moon, Kedar almost shouted,

"Now that would be a very bright phenomenon".

Joiada looked at the cluster, then at Spica, and followed with,

"It could happen if it follows the same pattern, then they would fall together, what date does the chart say they should fall"?

They all moved at once, Kedar uncovered the lantern to read with, Meres and Ashpenaz went to unroll the chart while Joiada made space on the little table that had been set up for them.

Ashpenaz found the dates of rising and falling and ran his shaking finger down to Spica but before he could read it Meres shouted,

"Near the end of Kislev". (December)

"That's five months, I wonder where it will have taken us by then"? Joiada added, he sounded all keyed up.

"You keep looking at your Scriptures Joiada, the answer is there somewhere" exclaimed Meres.

"We are well in front of the Cluster, that will give me more time to study them", returned Joiada, then as an afterthought, he said,

"Why don't you help me, they are written in Greek".

Greek had been the everyday language long before their schooldays, all were competent enough to read these new modern Scriptures Joiada had acquired.

Joiada now addressed his friends like a schoolmaster as he said,

"Up early in the morning, you will each be given one of the Prophets to read".

The other three looked at each other, then at Joiada and followed with,

"YES SIR"!

And so as ordered by their host the three of them assembled by the second hour (8 am) the following morning, each were given a manuscript to read.

"If you come across anything you think may be relevant" ordered Joiada in a jovial mood,

"Don't hesitate to mention it, happy hunting, or should I say reading".

As they settled down in the cloisters to their new task Ashpenaz quipped,

"It's a long time since we all swotted together".

"Good old days" added Meres.

A girl of fourteen came to them about an hour later with drinks, after attending to each one she went to Joiada and quietly asked,

"Will that be all Grandfather"?

He looked at her and winked as he replied, "You keep looking after us all day long my sweet little Miriam".

She bowed and smiled before leaving them.

Two hours went by before anyone spoke then Kedar broke the silence, he had been given the book of the Prophet Zechariah, he asked,

"This may be relevant Joiada, should I read it"?

"Certainly, let's hear it Kedar", prompted Joiada.

"The Lord will be King over the whole earth
On that day there will be one Lord
And His Name the only NAME ! Zech 14,9.

"That sounds appropriate, the Messiah will be King over all", commented Meres.

"I'm glad I've got all of you searching" said Joiada, "It looks as if there are quite a few references, it would take me ages to find them all".

They studied quietly, Miriam was on hand to keep them refreshed.

Ashpenaz was reading the Book of Daniel, another hour went by and he asked,

"Joiada, who are the saints"?

"People who are faithful and love our Lord God are called saints" answered Joiada reverently.

Although many local minor Kings and Tribal Chieftains had come to worship the God of Abraham for well over a hundred years, many would not be familiar with the word 'saint'.

Joiada invited him to share his find with them,

"Read what you've found Ashpenaz".

He responded,

But the Saints of the Most High Will receive the Kingdom
and will possess it for ever- yes for ever and ever". Dan 7,18.

"Everyone whoever lived that loved the Lord and worshiped Him are known as Saints. With you coming to ask me about The Messiah has prompted me to be more aware of the Scriptures, I've got to admit although I worshipped God I did not study the Scriptures as I might have done. I thank you for giving me a fresh understanding of my faith", Joiada said.

Meres' quiet voice followed with,

"It was meant to be that Kedar found the Star Cluster, I'd like to be a Saint".

"I never thought I would ever have such a feeling since we set out on this venture, but I've got to admit I feel so wonderful" added Ashpenaz.

"Coming from you, always full of action, you've never expressed such emotions before" said Joiada,

"This is all part and parcel of following Triune".

The four Princes returned to their studies of the Scriptures again and for half an hour or so all was quiet. ... suddenly Ashpenaz almost erupted with.

"I've found my name"!

He shouted with delight, then continued with, "I became interested in the Book of Daniel so I went to the beginning, it's about four young Jewish boys being taken to Babylon, the King put them in charge of his Chief Advisor, whose name was Ashpenaz".

He looked at them with a great big grin and added,

"He was chief Advisor to Nebuchadnezzar". (Daniel, 1.)

"All right, keep your beard on, that means we wont be able to talk to you for a week" said Kedar.

They were all very amused with Ashpenaz' finding his name.

It set Joiada thinking about it for a moment then he said,

"It is just like us, I'd forgotten about Daniel and his three companions, they were taken by King Nebucahdnezzar to be educated in the Babylonian schools so that they would become useful in advising him in Government. They were chosen because they were already well educated, I imagine for their ability to study".

"We came to study together in different circumstances, but you are right, four young friends together for five years or so, they would become eternal mates for ever, just like us" remarked Meres.

"Yes but I'd be the boss. Because it says so in the scriptures" Ashpenaz reminded them.

The other three found something to throw at him, their student days came flooding back as they once again enjoyed the camaraderie they had shared for so many years.

The day was much the same for the staff at the Caravansary, but the four Princes were so immersed in their studies they were totally unaware of time.

As the sun moved towards the horizon they automatically made their way to the platform to observe Triune.

They ascended the observation tower just as the sun set, some stars are quite bright in the twilight just before complete darkness.

The moon was almost full making another bright clear sky for their studies.

"If we don't find it in the Scriptures, we shall have to anticipate where to head for", Kedar remarked as he looked at his discovery.

"That's why I'd like to find a Prophecy relating to a definite place" added Joiada.

"I'm sure we can bide our time here for a few days, make a move again when it catches up with us" Ashpenaz said.

"I would say about five days and then move to be in front of it again", Meres added.

They all agreed, then Joiada mentioned something that they hadn't thought about,

"If we are still travelling when the rains begin towards the end of Cheshvan (October), there will be nights when it is obscure".

"We shall have to be on call throughout the night and let our servants fetch us if and when the sky becomes clear" replied Ashpenaz.

Wherever they travelled two attendants kept watch in turn throughout the night especially whenever they camped outdoors.

"Hopefully we will be able to keep track of it during the rains" said Meres.

"If we are still following when the winter sets in we could have some rough nights" warned Joiada.

They had made observations early again in order to continue searching the Scriptures for further clues so once again after their evening meal they made their way to the same study room as before.

Joiada had found something in Isaiah that he began the discussion with,

"The people walking in darkness,
Have seen a great light" Isa 9,2

"Surely that has a bearing on the future Son of God" declared Meres.

"I felt exactly the same when I first read it" answered Joiada.

"You can't imagine anything to do with God that is dark" Kedar commented.

"It only seems like yesterday that we were at Alexandria studying together, where have thirty years gone"? Ashpenaz asked rather perplexed.

"The God of Abraham is certainly very different from the Greek gods" Meres said.

"Or the Roman gods" added Ashpenaz.

"Their gods are mythological, a god for this and a god for that, where Abraham lived before he was called from Ur of the Chaldees, they worshipped the sun and the moon or the stars. The Egyptians did the same, that's why Abraham was called by what we believe to be the ONE and ONLY GOD." Joiada was adamant about His God.

A brief silence followed before Kedar asked tentatively,

"So you are pleased that we have come to get your attention to the expected coming of the Messiah, it seems as if you have learned something of the Scriptures yourself Joiada".

"You are right there" answered Joiada, my father is far more knowledgeable than me, he would have given me a telling off, he always said you are a very good business man but don't forget your Scriptures, I was taught many of these things we've discussed as a boy. But I must confess I'd forgotten them".

"Uncle Shadrach was right sending us here though, I'm glad to be reading your new Manuscripts" responded Ashpenaz.

Joiada answered with,

"Father had learned by rote far more than I did, but you have stirred me up so much with my interest in the expectation of a Messiah, that I think I would go to the ends of the earth to see this venture through".

Meres asked quietly,

"Why did God let Nebuchadnezzar conquer the Jews and take them into Exile"?

Although his family now believed in the God of Abraham, for many years he did not know much of the Jewish History. They had heard of Moses and some of the Great Jewish Kings but never had they been able to learn why God turned upon them to punish them so.

"If you would like a history in a nutshell I'll give you one" Joiada looked from one to the other and had a favourable response, so he began,

"One of Abraham's grandchildren, Joseph, was sold as a slave to Caravan Merchants and taken to Egypt".

Joiada looked at them hoping for a response.

"Joseph the dreamer" yelled Kedar.

"What happened to him"? asked Ashpenaz.

"He became next to the Pharaoh, and was put in charge of all the corn" replied Meres.

"You see, you know more than you thought" said Joiada raising his finger and pointing at them like a Pedagogue. Then he continued, "Joseph brought the whole of his family to live in Egypt which at that time was the whole Jewish Nation, only about seventy of them".

"How long were they there"? Ashpenaz asked.

"Four hundred years" came the reply, "The small number to begin with would be quite tolerable but after such a long time there were well over a million of them, the Egyptians became worried and decided to make them slaves in order to keep control over them".

"I suppose that's understandable" added Meres.

"We believe it was all in God's Divine Plan to make them a Great Nation", Joiada continued, "After four hundred years the present Pharaoh would not understand how important Joseph had been, the Jews were aliens to him".

"Didn't he want to get rid of them"? asked Kedar.

"Not at all, as slaves they were made to do the heavy work that no one else wanted to do, especially heavy laborious tasks in the building trade. Moving heavy stones into place and making bricks by the million" Joiada answered.

"Now I can recognise how he felt about keeping such a workforce" Meres added.

"He did try to stop them from multiplying, he made a decree that all male Hebrew babies were to be killed" Joiada informed them.

"Now I seem to recall the story of Moses being put in a basket and floated on the River Nile" added Meres, "But I couldn't remember why".

"Bits of the old stories are handed down and told to children but only parts are remembered, floating a baby in a basket on the river could be told to children for amusement" Joiada commented shrugging his shoulders, "And I imagine you can remember that Pharaoh's daughter was the one that found him and brought him up as a Royal Prince".

Joiada's three Royal friends now realised what had made Moses so different.

"Like us" exclaimed Ashpenaz, "He would have had the best Egyptian education possible, tuition in every subject, but if I recall he ran away from Egypt".

"Yes he had to" continued Joiada, "He saw one of his own people being ill treated by an Egyptian, he became so angry that he killed the taskmaster

involved, but then for some reason his own people turned against him, so he had to run away".

"What made his own people do such a thing"? asked Meres.

"God sometimes moves in a mysterious way but the outcome all fits his divine plan" answered Joiada, Moses went to live with a shepherd priest named Jethro, and eventually married his daughter".

Ashpenaz broke in with. "Didn't Moses see a bush on fire"?

"There, you see parts of the old stories are still in your mind, he did see a burning bush but the bush was not being consumed, so he went closer to investigate and he heard God call him by name".

"Just imagine" quipped Kedar, "I would have been scared stiff".

"Moses was told to take off his sandals, he was standing on

Holy Ground".

Joiada said solemnly.

"It's made me go all goose pimpled" declared Ashpenaz.

"So being confronted like that, Moses had no option but to do what he was told" added Meres.

"No, he actually told God he had the wrong man" said Joiada, apparently he stuttered, with some sort of speech impediment, and he didn't think he was capable enough to be sent to plead with Pharoah".

"Fancy telling God that He had chosen the wrong man for the job" said Kedar.

"I did say I would give you a brief version of our history so I'd better get on with it, as you know Moses did get to lead the Hebrews out of Egypt but only after a terrifying act of God", added Joiada.

"An angel of death went through the land, or something like that" said Meres quietly.

"After sending plagues, hoards of flies, frogs, locusts, nothing seemed to make Pharaoh agree to letting his Hebrew Slaves go, so God warned him that all first born animals, and humans would die if he did not let them go" said Joiada.

"And Pharaoh didn't believe him"? Meres asked.

"No, so the angel of death was sent" continued Joiada, "Even the Hebrews had to avoid it or they would have suffered the same fate, they were to kill a lamb and sprinkle some of it's blood on the door frame of their house, by so doing, the destroying angel 'passed over' them".

"And that is why you celebrate a meal each year called the Passover" said Kedar.

"That's correct, we have celebrated the Passover ever since" added Joiada, even Pharaoh lost his firstborn son. Very reluctantly he told the Hebrews to go, the Egyptians were now very much afraid, they even gave the Hebrews all manner of gifts in order to get them away, these gifts were used later".

"Between Egypt and Exile was a long time, where did they do wrong for God to punish them"? Meres asked.

"After they left Egypt, God met Moses on the top of Mount Sinai and gave him the Ten Commandments, the most important one is the first one, if you break that one you are in trouble" answered Joiada.

"I don't remember hearing what they were, or if I did I've forgotten" said Kedar.

"The first one is,

Thou shall love the Lord your God with all your might and Him only shalt thou serve",

Said Joiada dramatically.

"I can understand many people being tempted to follow other gods" commented Ashpenaz.

"There are no other gods, we must believe there is only one Supreme God and that's the God of Abraham" answered Joiada emphatically.

"Now it all adds up, Abraham was called to begin a New Race of people to prove to the world that there is only ONE GOD" declared Meres.

Joiada continued, "You must have heard that some people worship images made from wood, clay, all sorts of material, many Prophets were sent to warn the people not to bow down to an image that could not talk, hear, see or move. When you think of it, to do something like that is really senseless".

"Now you put it like that I have done some very silly things, I was in Jerash once and went into the Greek Temple of Artimis, I got carried away and bought a silver effigy to protect me" admitted Ashpenaz.

"Haven't we all" added Kedar.

Meres nodded in agreement.

"I'm not surprised that the Hebrews went off the rails at times" declared Ashpenaz.

"When they first went to Canaan they were tempted to follow the local people, their religions were very tempting, their gods were much freer, they allowed them to do things that Our God forbade them to do" said Joiada.

"So that is what it is all about, I can see now why they were taken into Exile" exclaimed Kedar.

"God sent many Prophets to warn them, He forgave them many times but as Isaiah says in his Book,

"All we like sheep have gone astray we have turned everyone to his own way. Isa 56,6" *quoted Joiada.*

"That has explained everything" commented Meres, "If you live according to God's Law, you have God's Blessing, but you are in trouble without it". Meres added lifting his hands in a gesture.

"I am so pleased that you can appreciate our way of life, although we are not as strict as other Jewish sects" said Joiada.

"Moses gave them the biggest warning of all before he died" he added.

"So Moses warned them as well as the Prophets"? Kedar exclaimed.

"Yes, he told them that they must choose life or death" said Joiada.

"He didn't pull any punches then did he, what were his actual words"? Meres asked.

Joiada looked very serious at each one of his friends in turn, then he bent down to his box and picked up what looked like a much older piece of manuscript to his new ones, he began to read,

"See, I set before you today life and prosperity,
or death and destruction, for I command you to
love the Lord your God, to walk in his ways,
decrees and laws, then you will live and increase
and the Lord your God will bless you in the land
you are entering to possess". Deut 30,15

Again Joiada looked at each in turn to await their comments.

"You knew that Prophecy before any others by the look of that old manuscript" Meres said in his quiet little voice.

"I ought to have known you would notice the difference Meres, all Jews are told how important it is to follow Moses' last instructions, as he said, to us it is life or death" answered Joiada.

"Now we know how they landed up in Exile" added Kedar.

"Do you believe a New Messiah will change how you live"? Meres asked.

Joiada had to think hard before he tried to give an answer, after a long pause he replied,

"I can't tell you exactly what will happen, I believe the nearest answer is that God is sending a new leader that all people of every race can follow, and if He is the Prince of Peace we will all be better off".

Another pause then Meres said, "We can't wish for anything greater than that can we"?

"On that note my Royal friends, we will retire to reflect on what we have found" answered Joiada.

They certainly had many new thoughts to ponder in their minds as they retired for the night.

An early call for an hour before sunrise found them up on the platform with their instruments ready to see how far Triune had moved.

As predicted it had moved slightly nearer to Spica.

The Constellation of Virgo looked as if it would eventually have the company of Triune.

Ashpenaz was the first to comment, "Its still on this course to conjoin with Spica, and we all know how spectacular it will be if it does" he exclaimed.

"Indeed it will, if it continues on its present course" agreed Joiada.

"Then it will definitely go down in the western sky in the month of Tevet" (December) said Kedar.

"You must be proud Kedar, we could have missed all this" Meres reminded him.

"I can't believe how Blessed we are" added Joiada.

Just at that moment while they stood looking at Triune, the annual meteor shower gave one if it's displays.

Suddenly around Triune appeared a myriad of coloured lights that seemed to cascade towards the earth as if to herald the new star cluster.

Every year meteor showers can be seen around 12-13 of August, they look like tiny specks of coloured lights falling out of the sky.

Meres almost shouted, "What a magnificent sight to behold, we will remember that for ever".

"Forever and forever" they all shouted.

They stood staring in amazement until the sun came up to hide all the stars.

Joiada had informed Eli to take charge of all business deals to enable him to concentrate completely on their project with the stars.

Later he sat with his Royal guests as they reclined around a low table enjoying the morning meal.

Their experience seeing the meteor shower was still vivid in their minds.

"Do you think Joiada", asked Meres, "That the Messiah will arrive somewhere in Judea"?

Joiada took his time replying, he was putting his thoughts together.

Eventually, he said,

"There are more Jewish Sects other than the Judeans. Babylonians, Alexandrians and those on the Island of Elephantine.(on the River Nile) Not counting my Sect the Samaritans, but I'm sure it will be close to Jerusalem where Abraham is closely associated".

Meres looked at him and said,

"I thought you would come to that conclusion, if it does we must be ready to go much further south".

Joiada replied,

"Even our Journey is tied with Abraham, he travelled from Ur to Bethel near the border between Judea and Samaria".

"That will mean going into Herod's territory" said Ashpenaz gravely.

Suddenly a solemn ambience descended upon them.

King Herod the Great had a terrible reputation. He had usurped the Throne of David, he was made King of Judea through his ties with Rome, but he was ruthless, many of his own family had been eliminated in his climb to be King. He was an Idomean, but his father was partly Jewish and had adopted the Jewish way of life. Because Herod did not have much Jewish blood, he was hated by the Jews he ruled over.

However, Rome had the final say so the Jews could do nothing but accept him.

In order to appease them, Herod went on a building spree of such magnificence, they tolerated his efforts in trying to please them.

Work on a New Temple at Jerusalem had been in progress for fifteen years, the bulk of the work of The Temple itself was complete, the refinements and the great courtyard would not be finalised for many more years.

One thousand priests had been trained as stonemasons and builders because the Jews would not allow other men to work on the Holy Site.

Two thousand other workers and one thousand carts, moved the stone blocks from the quarry.

The stone in the local quarries was like white marble.

It turned to a golden creamy colour over the years.

Every block was quarried and finished before being moved to the Temple Site in order to keep the noise away from the sacred area.

The south wall was built up from the bottom of the Kidron valley to make a large outdoor platform area to accommodate Gentiles.

Some of the base blocks measured forty feet long and weighed over one hundred tons.

When completed it was a spectacular fete of engineering.

"I suppose we have all seen the new Temple" said Joiada

"Whoever sees that has to stop and admire it" said Ashpenaz.

"You *will* go there if we have to won't you Joiada"? Kedar asked.

Joiada did not answer immediately, his mind buzzed with what he knew about Herod. After much thought he said,

"Certainly, but I shall keep a low profile, you three will be able to roam freely, I have many business contacts there, but I try to avoid Herod" added Joiada.

"I picked up that he is not popular" commented Meres.

"We Samaritans are frowned upon by most of the Jewish hierarchy" said Joiada and followed with,

"But Herod's Jewish blood is very much thinner than mine".

At that Joiada guffawed loudly and this brought a happier tone back to their conversation.

Meres' mind had been racing ahead with the mention of Jerusalem which was much further to the south, it prompted him to say,

"I think it would be wise to keep our position way in front of Triune until we either find a clue in the Prophecies or anything else that could be relevant".

"I agree, we don't want to be caught out Meres, at the moment we command a good position but we must anticipate in good time to enable us to move fast enough if it becomes necessary" exclaimed Joiada.

"You said Herod had usurped the Throne of David" commented Meres.

"The Messiah will be in the line of David, God promised David the Throne would always be in his family" declared Joiada.

"Family records mean a great deal to Hebrews, I used to do business with a Jewish family who were always quoting their family history" said Ashpenaz,

"I wonder what Herod's family history would look like" he added.

Joiada gave a cynical laugh before replying,

"Herod gave orders that all the Jews should burn their family records".

"Wow, no wonder he is not popular" commented Ashpenaz.

"So there is a star connection, isn't the six pointed star David's symbol"? Meres asked.

"Indeed, it is also the symbol of all Jews" remarked Joiada.

"I'm sure I've seen a five pointed star as I've been on my

travels" Kedar reminded them.

"You are very observant Kedar", chuckled Joiada, "That is the star of Solomon".

"Said to be the wisest man that ever lived" quoted Meres.

"He was very wise, but he went off the rails, that's why the Kingdom was taken away from him because he broke the first Commandment".

Joiada had adopted his serious voice once again.

"I am surprised" said Ashpenaz, "We have always thought he was above reproach".

"He married many wives and had hundreds of concubines, but that was not his worst sin" added Joiada.

"He must have worshipped other gods" said wise Meres pointing a finger in the air.

"Some of his wives worshipped Baal and other deities, he was tempted and fell into the trap, he broke the most important Law that God gave us" replied Joiada.

"I wonder what sort of Messiah will be sent in order to make us free from sin" asked Meres.

The four Princes were oblivious to the hustle and bustle of Caravan business that continued around them, it was as if they were the only four people on earth. Their minds were full only of thoughts alluding to the pursuit of following Triune.

Joiada suddenly thought of something and went off inside without a word.

Kedar, Ashpenaz and Meres were left sitting in the shade of the cloisters, a gentle breeze made the heat more bearable as they mulled over the morning Scripture lesson.

Minutes later Joiada returned and made everyone in the quadrangle turn to look at him as he shouted,

"EUREKA, I've found it".

He came running over to them holding one of his manuscripts in the air.

He sat down among them and waited a second to get his breath back, he then spoke almost in a whisper,

"Bethlehem".

They were somewhat surprised at the mention of a village that they had heard very little about.

Meres then asked quietly with a curious look on his face,

"Aren't there two Bethlehems"?

"Trust you to think of both of them, but you are quite right as usual there are two" Joiada replied, then added with a smile,

"But it does state which one".

"How did you find it"? Ashpenaz asked.

"The last time you each had a manuscript I placed the sheets in the box as you handed them to me without putting them in number order, later when I picked up the box to do so, the one at the top was one of the Minor Prophets, Micah", replied Joiada.

"What made you start with that instead of putting them in order first"? Kedar asked.

"I just don't know, I picked it up and thought, I might as well start with this, I got to chapter five, and there it was,

But you Bethlehem, Ephrathah, though you are
Small among the clans of Judah
Out of you will come for me One who will be
Ruler over Israel.
He will stand and shepherd His flock
In the strength of The Lord." Mic 5,2

Silence for a moment before Meres spoke,

"That is why Triune is moving southwest".

Joiada lifted a finger, pointed at Meres and replied,

"Of course, it all fits, now we can adjust our route to arrive at Bethlehem".

"If Triune continues at the same speed we have plenty of time" added Kedar.

"Plenty of time to plan as we go" Joiada said,

"Just observe as often as we can in order to be on the safe side".

"You've soon got that worked out, but it sounds good to me" Kedar exclaimed.

"I'm so pleased uncle Shadrach suggested coming to you, but I

have the feeling we are being led by a much Higher Authority"
Ashpenaz said.

Each of the four Princes nodded in agreement.

When they were gathered together for the afternoon meal the
latest Prophecy Joiada had found gave them plenty to think about.

They tried to chat about other things while they ate but no
matter how they tried they came back to Triune.

Meres asked quietly,

"Will you go with us to Jerusalem or will you stay outside".

Joiada smiled at Meres, he had been thinking about that and
added,

"I believe that you should seek an audience with Herod for the
sake of protocol, we could upset him if we go so close to Jerusalem,
the local people may tip him off that a group of aristocratic
personnel have been by without him knowing, he would not be
pleased" replied Joiada seriously.

Meres suggested,

"You are right, we must not upset Herod, we will seek an
audience with him to ask his advice"

"I pick up that you must have had a disagreement with him at
sometime" Kedar commented.

Joiada looked at him for a moment then replied,

"Herod has rebuilt a lot of Samaria and many of the new
comers, mainly Greeks and Romans, are very pleased with what he
has done. Like the Jerusalem Temple, some very impressive
buildings such as Temples to other gods, are magnificent" replied
Joiada then added,

"One of his heathen buildings was to be built near one of our
Synagogues, we tried to get it moved further away but he took no
notice, he would not listen".

They sympathised with him, Ashpenaz asked,

"I suppose he likes to please the Greeks, are there many of
them"?

"Greece was over populated, and after Alexander took over
many saw the opportunity to emigrate, especially the wealthy ones,
of course they were the most influential. Later the wealthy Romans

did the same".

Meres quietly added,

"We all followed the new way of life, when the Cities of the Decapolis were built they were like a magnet to young people living in the surrounding areas, they could go and earn much more money.

Entertainment in the arenas and gymnasiums became another great attraction to them".

Joiada looked at each in turn and smiled as he said,

"We wouldn't be here how if we hadn't studied at the Alexander Academy would we", and he put his hand on each of their shoulders.

"We hold our heritage very dear to our hearts" exclaimed Ashpenaz,

"But we cannot stand in the way of progress, nor would we want to" he added.

"We will meet after sunset and study Triune, Eli will have everything ready for us" Joiada said as he began to pack his Scriptures away.

"Can't wait" said Kedar as he went off chuckling.

There was no moon as they prepared to study the night sky but as usual at this time of the year there was very little cloud.

The brightest star in the sky was Sirius. It was very prominent towards the eastern sky.

It prompted Ashpenaz to comment,

"The Egyptians will be over their New Year celebrations now, the Nile will be in full flood".

"It is the highlight of their year when Sirius rises" added Kedar.

"When you think of how important the Flood Waters are to them you can understand their passion, it produces abundant food for their coffers" added Meres.

Ashpenaz laughed loudly as he thought about what the Greeks said when Sirius rose, it prompted him to say,

"In Greece it is the start of 'dog days', when summer plants wilt, men weaken, and women are roused".

"Trust you to bring frivolity to the proceedings" said Joiada but like the others he had to chuckle.

When Triune had first appeared the three stars were quite dim but now they were quite easily found.

"I've picked Triune out without using the dioptra" said Kedar

The others looked up in the sky and agreed.

"That proves how much brighter it is since you first found it Kedar" said Meres.

After studying it with the apparatus it proved without doubt that it was almost level with the star Danebola.

Every time they studied Triune their enthusiasm was deepened, they became more engrossed in their endeavour to follow wherever it took them, even to the ends of the earth.

"We can definitely see that it is heading towards Spica unless it changes course" Kedar almost shouted with delight.

"This *has* to be the sign that we have all been waiting for" exclaimed Joiada, "It couldn't be alluding to any other happening or person but Our Messiah ".

Meres and Ashpenaz did not speak, they could not take their eyes away from Triune.

The whole starry sky all seemed to be radiating with an unusual aura, the four Princes felt they were the only people in the world that had been given the privilege of gazing at Triune's glory.

Joiada suddenly shouted,

'Praise Him, all you shining stars'

Meres said quietly,

"That has to be a quote from Scripture".

"Yes" replied Joiada "it is from Psalm 148 verse 3".

"I have not felt so moved in all my life" said Joiada as he looked at his friends.

Ashpenaz felt his face and answered,

"Do I look as if I'm glowing, my face feels as if it is burning".

"I thought it was just me" said Meres.

Kedar looked at them for a second, then grinned as he said,

"I hope you're not going to blame me".

Without thinking Joiada reached out and took Ashpenaz and Kedar by the hand, automatically Meres also reached for their other hands.

As they stood in a circle they knew the mission they had embarked upon was indeed, The Lord God's special assignment.

It was an hour after their usual time before they sat around the low table for supper.

They ate very quietly, hardly speaking,

Joiada was already sorting manuscripts out before he had finished.

"When I found the Prophecy about Bethlehem, I did not take much notice of the lines that followed but I have thought about them since. The Hebrews were taken into Exile for punishment, but as they turned back to God, they were allowed to return and slowly get back into the Temple Worship they had always known".

Joiada enlightened them by reading out the rest of the Prophecy.

"Therefore Israel will be abandoned until the time
when she who is in labour gives birth and the rest
of his brothers return to join the Israelites". Mic 5,3

"I think that's very relevant, it has to be alluding to the Virgin Birth surely, but I can understand you only seeing the Bethlehem lead" said Meres.

"I knew you would understand how I came to dwell on the town of Bethlehem, but I suddenly realised the importance of the whole Prophecy".

"How long do we have before Triune goes down Meres"? asked Ashpenaz.

"According to the charts not till Tevet" (December) Meres replied.

"With Triune moving so slowly it is giving us plenty of time to get acquainted with your history", declared Meres.

"I'm enjoying learning about your past since the time of Abraham's calling" said Ashpenaz.

"Certainly" added Kedar, "We have heard names of great men that your God called to lead the Jews from time to time, but to have it explained why and how, it gives a sense of belonging now we share your God".

Joiada was taken aback by Kedar's comments.

He replied,

"I'm overwhelmed", he paused for a moment and continued, "Fancy you wanting to know about our past, It's made me very aware that you have come to worship our God, but for wanting to be so involved as you are with the coming of the Messiah, it has really moved me".

"I feel the same" added Meres, "It has brought us so much nearer to your God, I also wish to learn more".

Again Joiada looked from one to the other rather dumbfounded before replying,

"You should be using the term, 'Our God' when you speak to me instead of, 'Your God'".

"That will be an honour" added Meres,

"We can all use the term, 'OUR GOD'".

One by one they repeated, "Our God".

"I have this great feeling" said Joiada "That the Messiah will be for all people on earth, it goes with the theme that began with Abraham when God made a covenant with him".

"You must tell us about that" exclaimed Meres.

"God said to him.

'One day all people on earth will be blessed through you" replied Joiada.

Meres was thinking almost out loud as he said,

"God told Abraham, not just the Hebrews, but all people on earth"? he queried

"Do you have any idea when"? Kedar asked.

"Not a clue" returned Joiada,

"I'm as much in the dark as you".

"It's all in God's plan, he told Abraham what would happen, that was nearly two thousand years ago, it will all happen in time".

"I'm sure you're right there Meres" declared Joiada "

"That could all fit in with The Messiah being heralded in the stars" said Kedar.

They all nodded in agreement, it prompted Joiada to say,

"I think we have more than enough to retire on for tonight,

ponder on your new studies, we will have a call before dawn to have a look at Triune's progress".

Very little else was mentioned.

Their thoughts and feelings were enough to dwell on as they made their way to their beds.

Soon after the morning call came, they were making their way up the observation platform.

Astronomers were a very special people.

Having the first blessing of strong eyesight, they would also need to have an intelligent, active mind and memory to retain where and when each star would rise and fall during the annual cycle.

It is little wonder that Astronomers were always near to kings and rulers to guide them and give advice in governing their domains.

The title 'Wise Men' was very appropriate.

Now they could pick out Triune by looking directly up into the sky they stood together in silence.

"What a wonderful discovery you made Kedar" said Joiada.

"If I hadn't, I'm sure one of you would have", answered Kedar.

The elite little group of Princes automatically felt the bond between them was becoming stronger each time they looked up at Triune.

As they sat in the cloisters after breakfast they put their individual points of view forward as to the next plan of action.

"We could make our way slowly and make camp each night or stay here a few days more, either way we can follow Triune's progress. You are most welcome to my hospitality as long as you wish" invited Joiada.

"It will be three or four nights before it's overhead, I wouldn't mind staying two more days and then moving on, we are very blessed with your hospitality, but I am also enjoying your history lessons" retorted Meres.

This brought laughter from the others, Joiada grinned as he said,

"It seems to me you wish to become fully fledged proselytes".

"As opposed to ordinary Gentiles" added Ashpenaz

Joiada was quiet for a moment, he was mulling over something he had mentioned a little earlier.

"Have you forgotten something Joiada"? asked Ashpenaz.

"I mentioned the route we are following, and how very significant it is to all Jews" answered Joiada.

"Because of Abraham" remarked Kedar.

"Much more then that, Abraham came first from Ur, he would have come by Nippur where our Convention was held, he went further north into Haran, but then was redirected south which would put him back on our route" added Joiada.

"I see what you mean" said Meres.

"Yes, but there are many more instances that are related" stated Joiada, he continued, "Jacob, Abraham's grandson was sent to Paddan Arram to find a wife among close relatives, he returned to Canaan where they lived until Joseph was taken to Egypt."

"Moses brought them back again" Kedar said.

Ashpenaz suddenly shouted,

"Until they were taken into Exile".

"Quite right, and which way did they go"? Joiada asked.

"Back along the same route to Babylon" answered Meres.

"Then they came by this way when they returned to Jerusalem, this route has been used by Jews so much" then Joiada looked at each in turn and added,

"Now Triune is taking us along the same path".

"It does seem more than a coincidence" said Ashpenaz.

"Over all those years it has brought riches beyond measure carrying the valuable cargos through each country it traverses".

"My wife and daughters are enjoying the fashionable silk garments that are now all the rage" said Joiada.

"You mean the Chinese silk that is flowing along this route, It seems the big cities can't get enough of it.

We have silk adorning our Princely turbans and tunics, you have to agree it adds a certain panache",

said Ashpenaz who's tall lithe figure always attracted much attention when so attired.

"There is another commodity that is transported but it is usually concealed" whispered Meres.

"You mean precious stones" added Joiada,

"They usually end up with the person that pays the highest price".

"Talking of that sort of cargo, Eli told me this morning that we could expect a visit from King Phraates' Custom's Inspectors, they pay a visit every few months" added Joiada.

"Are they difficult to please"? asked Kedar.

"No, I try to keep everything the right side of the law, if we suspect anything with travellers or Caravan Leaders, we tell them the King's men are not far away, any shady characters either leave or keep well out of sight" said Joiada.

"No doubt if they know you don't tolerate anything underhand, it keeps them in order" said Meres.

"The Authorities make enough from Trade Routes, they just come and show their faces, if they are happy we are happy" concluded Joiada.

As usual Meres had been mulling it over as he listened, he said quietly,

"And now Triune is using the Trade Route and will bring riches to all mankind".

"I'm sure you're right Meres, " remarked Kedar.

"It will bring more than riches", exclaimed Joiada.

They set off two days later to continue their journey.

Just before the sunrise they were crossing the Euphrates River over the bridge controlled by Macedonian Aristocracy.

Joiada gave details of their party to the Officer at the check point, like most Merchant Traders he was well known at all Border controls.

Dura-Europos had been built on an escarpment almost ninety metres above the River which meant going down a fairly steep section of road after leaving the complex taking them directly through the City as they followed the road leading to Palmyra.

This was the next long stretch of their Journey.

"Another big city that brought wealth to many local lads" exclaimed Kedar as he looked at the large impressive buildings they were riding by.

Dura-Europos was known as the Pompeii of the desert, over the years it has yielded deep secrets to the spades of American Archaeologists. The oldest synagogue in the world was brought from here by the Yale University Expedition and rebuilt in the Damascus Museum.

After crossing the river, the route to Palmyra veered southwest away from the River Euphrates.

However, caravan traffic still abounded.

The thoughts of moving nearer their goal gave them an elated air as the camels trekked along in silence.

Four Royal Princes, but they were human beings when all said and done, how did they come to be on such an expedition to go looking for the Messiah.

Unexpectedly, they had become four very special Royal Princes on their way to pay homage to THE KING OF KINGS.

What a great privilege that God had chosen them for this great commission.

Each began to wonder whether they were having the dream of a lifetime.

On a journey to see the Prince of Peace, THE SON of GOD.

Suddenly they were brought back to reality.

At a fast gallop, a group of horses came by at such a pace it seemed as if they were standing still.

They were jogging steady at five miles an hour, the horsemen went by almost twenty miles an hour and were soon out of sight.

"Romans again" shouted Joiada.

"No doubt scouting to see which way the land lies" added Ashpenaz.

"They would like to spread their wings further but even Rome has to tread carefully in some areas" said Kedar.

"We shall end up in their territory eventually" said Meres.

"It doesn't seem credible to think we are on such a pursuit that will end up in the jurisdiction of Rome" stated Ashpenaz.

"More to the point" broke in Joiada, "Under the terrible Herod who rules for Rome".

This ended the conversation for the moment.

Again they realised how upset Joiada was about Herod's rule.

After leaving the city they could travel faster, two hours later they stopped at a clump of trees during the hottest part of the day.

This was a leisurely way to travel that was easy both for men and animals, but it still kept them well in front of Triune.

After refreshments prepared by their attendants they rested as they discussed what they may encounter.

"What are your thoughts about the Romans Joiada"? asked Kedar.

Joiada mulled over the question for a moment, then answered,

"Like the Greeks, they have brought a new way of life to add to what the Greeks left behind. Advanced science is useful as long as they allow us to live our own life style, like all new bosses we are expected to knuckle under and conform to legislation".

Joiada's tone of voice was enough for them to pick up some resentment.

"Have you had to do anything you did not want to do"? asked Meres.

Joiada was very quiet for a few moments, he then answered with a question. "Didn't you notice I was a few hours late in joining you at the Convention"?

"We assumed it was business that had held you up" commented Ashpenaz.

"Nothing of the sort" Joiada replied indignantly,

"I can arrange my sons and many other members of the family to take care of business now, would you believe it, I had to go and register where I was born".

"The Census" Meres almost cried out,

"Don't tell me you had to register personally".

"What Census" asked Ashpenaz frowning.

"Caesar Augustus decreed that every one under Roman Rule was to travel to the place where their family line is on record and register for the population to be counted" replied Joiada. "This includes young and old of all ages, fortunately I only had to travel to Samaria but some people have had to travel very long distances according to where their Family is registered".

Now they understood why Joiada was so incensed.

"I get on well with most of them, they have had quite a few horses from our Stud Farm, mainly the Cicilian stock that we breed, very much sort after. The Romans are willing to pay good prices, but to be ordered about can be annoying", Joiada added.

"Was there a set date" asked Kedar.

"As near to last Tevet, (December) as they could get" Joiada answered.

"In all lands occupied by Rome" Ashpenaz ventured to ask.

Joiada nodded slowly before he replied. "For weeks we saw families of all kinds walking or riding donkeys to the Register Office where their Family Chieftain had been originally recorded".

The three Royal Princes could hardly believe what Joiada had just told them.

It was obvious why he was so resentful.

"We had just returned home to 'Freedom', our Estate just outside Samaria and saw a couple go by on the way to Bethlehem, she was riding an old donkey as her husband walked along with it. I asked them to come and rest awhile, and join us for some refreshments", Joiada informed them.

"Did they say where they were from" asked Meres.

"He was a carpenter from Nazareth" replied Joiada and then added,

"She was expecting a child, they had travelled most of the day, my wife Ruth was so anxious about her we gave them shelter for the night".

"They would have at least two more days Journey" said Kedar.

"I swapped their donkey for a younger one before they went off the following morning, Ruth gave them more food to take with them, we often wondered how they had fared the rest of the Journey".

They each pondered among themselves what the outcome would be for the couple.

Then they had a doze as they rested in the heat of the day.

When the sun was going down, their attendants began to set up the travelling gear used for studying the stars whilst on the move.

A tripod with a dioptra to be fixed on top was set up, this enabled them to hold everything steady while taking a fixed bearing on any star in the night sky.

Kedar was the first there, after taking a reading he shouted,

"The three stars are closer and brighter than ever"

Meres looked through the dioptra and added,

"Now it is level with Danebola".

Ashpenaz pushed forward to have a look.

"It's just as if the other stars are all responding", he said.

Joiada took his turn to look at Triune.

"You are right Ashpenaz, all the *stars* are welcoming the Messiah".

Their mounts were soon ready to ride in the moonlight, they were going to travel for three hours and then settle for the night.

Fifteen miles further they dismounted near some trees where there was a spring. All such facilities were marked for all travellers to take advantage of.

Meres thought if he asked Joiada more about the Scriptures it would help to put his mind in a happier mood.

"Have you thought of, or found any more relevant prophecies Joiada"?

After a moment Joiada replied,

"I had a thought about something I was taught as a boy and it had slipped my mind until I picked up one of my old scrolls, after reading it I thought it was very relevant".

His three friends each turned to look at him, he went on,

"Moses was talking to the Hebrews about their future.

He told them,

"The Lord your God will raise up for you a Prophet like me from among your own brothers.

You must listen to Him". Deut 18,16.

"So if someone like Moses was to follow later, it would have to be another great Prophet" said Meres, and followed with, "Or someone Greater".

"If they had", Joiada hesitated, he seemed to change his mind,

"I should say, if we had a leader like Moses, we should not be under Roman Rule".

Although Meres had tried to get Joiada to change the subject, both he and the other two realised how it must be the top of his mind.

Kedar tried a different approach of changing the subject.

"Since our days at the Academy, we have applied our studies well, each of us has done well for our Families, especially you Joiada, you must be proud of what you have achieved, whether under Roman Rule or not" Ashpenaz said adamantly.

He really admired Joiada's family the way they had become such an important part of the Caravan Industry.

Meres added,

"We are proud to be your associates Joiada, your name carries a lot of weight wherever it is mentioned, you said yourself the Romans wanted some of your horses".

Joiada was looking down, slowly he began to smile as he looked up at them. Then he said,

"With comrades like you, what does it matter about Romans being in charge".

"We three are not under them at the moment, but who can predict the future, kingdoms come and kingdoms go" said Ashpenaz.

Meres reminded them of something they had heard at the Academy,

"The great Historian, Herodotus said, 'the people of the land stand by and observe the passing antics of rulers and armies'".

Palmyra

Mild He lays His glory by, Born, that man no more may die;
Born, to raise the sons of earth; Born, to give them second birth.
(C Wesley)

After a long weary trek along the route from Dura-Europos, Palmyra was a very welcome sight.

It was known as 'The Bride of the Desert', two rivers were close by, palm trees grew in profusion almost everywhere, hence it's name.

Many Trade Routes intersected here and converged into an avenue that had three hundred and fifty columns alongside.

It was one of the richest cities in the near east. Solomon first built a city here known as Tadmor.

Egyptian and Persian charioteers came to buy the much sort after Cilician Bred horses, at Solomon's famous Stud Farm.

The queen of Sheba was also a visitor here.

Now it had become Hellenised, it was an important City of the Decapolis, but it was not to come under Roman Rule until 50 AD.

The entourage of the four Princes made their way through this magnificent city almost to the other side before they came to yet another Caravansary belonging to Joiada's Family.

News of their arrival was known a few minutes before they made an entry into the quadrangle and as before, all the staff that were not busy with a task, ran out to welcome Joiada and his Royal party.

The staff stood in a long line twenty-five or so in all, with heads bowed.

In front of them, near the main doorway, stood a very tall figure dressed in a dazzling set white of clothes which seemed to radiate the morning sunlight like a mirror.

His gold coloured silken turban was set with precious stones, almost like a sparkling light above his aged bearded face.

It was uncannily silent as they made their way to this person standing so erect, and so immaculately arrayed.

After Joiada's camel had knelt, he alighted and slowly made his way to this ominous figure in silence.

As he approached, it almost seemed as if the world had stood still.

When he was six feet away he stopped and bowed very low.

The tall man nodded slightly and spoke,

"It is a great pleasure to see you Joiada my son, when you are refreshed, bring the Royal Princes to our guest room and tell me all about this special mission King Shadrach has enlightened me with".

Then he put his arms gently around Joiada and hugged him for a brief moment.

He turned to the Princes and added, "Please enter and make yourselves at home my Royal Guests" and he made a small bow towards them.

After they had dismounted they bowed and thanked King Nathan for his special royal welcome.

Joiada's father was the King of his Tribe, he was a very respected but well loved King. Obviously he had received news of their mission from King Shadrach who had always been a great friend and ally when in need.

He was a little older than Shadrach but still led an active life.

A messenger had brought this news three weeks ahead of them, not having the need to stop only for rest or refreshments.

His instructions had been to call at Palmyra and check if King Nathan was here, if not to go to Damascus.

An hour later they were received in a sumptuous guest room. He was seated on a lavish armchair set facing and in front of four other plush chairs. These were arranged around a low table with drinks and choice fruit.

"Please be seated my young Princes, I've been waiting with bated breath to hear all about this new find amongst the heavenly bodies that you study so ardently".

From the tone of his voice they could tell how eager he was to hear more since he had been informed.

The King was quite envious although he did not show it. He knew they had been able to study under the most eminent teachers in the known world.

The education they had received was the best available when they were students.

Their love of Astronomy added to this envy, because most of all Nathan had not been so blest with suitable strong eyesight.

He could only look up for a few minutes at the stars before his eyes watered and his vision became blurry.

This was the real reason for his envy, he realised he had missed out from being able to study the wonderful world of the heavenly bodies.

However, he didn't like to make it known why he did not study the stars, he let them think he was not clever enough to remember the names and where they were to be found.

"What information did King Shadrach send Father"? Joiada inquired.

King Nathan gestured with his hands and with a radiant smile he replied excitedly,

"His message revealed wonderful news", the Kings eyes seemed to be open twice their usual size as he waited with baited breath.

"My Lord King", Ashpenaz intervened respectfully, "Uncle Shadrach was convinced of it before we left him, but since we have followed and observed the Cluster, we are sure that it must be the sign of a great happening".

"Also Joiada has enlightened us with your Holy Scriptures, my Lord" added Meres.

This pleased Nathan even more, he turned to Kedar and said,

"I also understand that we have to thank Kedar for finding it".

Kedar was a little embarrassed and replied,

"My Lord King, I consider myself very fortunate to have found it, it could have been any of us".

"Humble Kedar, obviously our Lord God chose you" said the King, then asked,

"What Scriptures have you discussed Joiada"?

Joiada smiled at his father, he knew he would be pleased with his answer and replied,

"Your favourite saying was the first one I told them".

Nathan's face lit up again with a smile, he lifted his hands in the air and recited as if he was giving a rendition to the whole world.

"For I am coming to live among you", then he adjusted his tone and continued, "From the Prophet Zechariah, what a wonderful way to begin learning our Scriptures".

Then the King adopted a much more serious look and followed with,

"You all seem very sure about this assignment you have undertaken, even King Shadrach" then added with a hint of envy,

"He has seen this sign among the stars with you".

Joiada noticed his friends were a little puzzled, they were not aware of the King's inability to stare at the stars long enough to be able to sort out which was which.

"May I clarify the situation Father"?

The King looked at them kindly and said,

"Please do Joiada, it would be best for them to know".

"Father's eyes are not so strong as ours" Joiada told them, he has never been able to stare at the stars longer than a few minutes before his eyes get blurred".

"Do not be sorry for me" said the King, "I am very blessed with all the faculties I do have, it just means that you must tell me everything from the very beginning of Kedar's first sighting, we will have a meal and rest and resume again this evening".

Joiada and his friends stood and after paying homage to the King they withdrew to their guest quarters.

Nathan knew they would be anxious to observe the position of Triune after sunset, he asked them to bring the chart after plotting it's present location so they could show him the very latest progress of Triune.

Almost six hours later, the King met them in the same room for a full report.

More oil lights had been set out than usual to give extra light in order to aid Nathan to study the charts.

He wanted to be able to comprehend the full significance of this wonderful happening regardless of not being able to see the actual event in the sky.

Nathan could hardly wait for them to arrange lights around the charts for him.

When they were ready, Joiada made room for him to stand in the centre position in order to explain just what was different.

With being so tall, the King could quite easily tower above the charts on display.

A small rough circle had been formed from a papyrus reed and was placed on the chart around the Constellation of Leo.

"My father, this chart shows the usual layout of Leo and Leo minor, without the new stars" said Joiada as he pointed them out on the first chart.

Nathan bent down quite close, it was obvious his old eyes were not as good as he would have liked them to be. After a few minutes he remarked,

"I suppose the larger dots are the brighter stars, the tiny dots are stars not so bright, is that right Joiada"?

"You are quite right my father, now look at the new chart, it shows where Kedar first saw it, and again to the new position it has moved to since then".

Joiada unrolled a smaller chart and placed it over Leo, this was a replica of Leo but the new stars had been drawn in.

The King scrutinised the smaller chart, after a few moments he said,

"Kedar must have been clever to notice such small stars" exclaimed Nathan.

"I don't know how he did notice them" added Meres, "When he first pointed them out to me, I could only just see them".

"We always said he had the best eyes of the four of us" commented Ashpenaz.

"So what do they look like now"? asked the King.

"This is tonight's observation" said Joiada as he replaced the small chart with the latest one.

This now showed Triune in line with the bright Regulas. The three stars were almost as bright, also they were noticeably closer together.

After studying the latest chart the King looked up at the four Princes, he could hardly believe the difference from the first chart. He was speechless for a moment.

Then he went and sat down, again without a word.

No one spoke, they waited for the King's observation.

He sat looking at the charts on the table, gradually he looked up at them and said very quietly.

"No wonder Shadrach told you to follow the stars".

He paused a moment then added

"It has to be pointing to the Messiah".

The four Princes sat down quietly one by one.

Meres was the first to speak in that quiet voice of his,

"What I can't understand is how Kedar was the one to notice it" then he followed with,

"We are not Hebrews".

The King looked at Meres for a moment, gradually a smile formed on the old Kings kindly face as he replied,

"I understand Joiada has been enlightening you with our scriptures, I wonder whether he has told you Isaiah's Prophecy that could explain your thoughts".

Joiada looked at his father and asked with respect,

"Which one would that be, my Lord"?

Nathan quoted,

'I will make you a light for the Gentiles, that you
may bring my Salvation to the ends of the earth'. Isa 49,6.

Silence followed while each one pondered deeply about this latest Prophecy.

Eventually Kedar was prompted to ask,

"Do you think my Lord King, that Gentiles will benefit from this new Messiah"?

Nathan thought long and hard before answering, he had studied the history of the Jews like every other Jewish boy and many times he had wondered about the way things had changed since Abraham had been called.

After a few minutes he addressed them,

"There were twelve Tribes of Israel after Moses had led them out of Egypt, but after Solomon died, because of his sin, ten tribes were taken from Judah but later they also sinned that's why they were taken away to Babylon".

"Joiada has mentioned that my Lord King, we found it difficult to understand" said Ashpenaz.

The King looked surprised, "You have covered some ground in your studies" he replied, he turned to Joiada and said,

"You have done well Joiada, you must have had many sessions with our Scriptures".

"Because we travelled faster than Triune, we had time waiting for it to catch us up".

Replied Joiada, he was pleased that his father was so impressed, he said,

"The LXX copy from Alexandria has been very enlightening, with it being written in Greek they have been reading it themselves".

King Nathan smiled at Joiada and said,

"You always had a way of organising to get the best results from people" then he looked at the others, winked his eye, and said,

"He's always been bossy since he was a very little boy".

This made them laugh, but Meres was prompted to say,

"I for one have felt very privileged to be allowed to study your history, I'm sure it would never have been allowed in the past".

The King answered again with a smile,

"I am so pleased you feel that way, I have had a copy of the LXX delivered to all our Caravansaries, and family homes, it is good to have our history recorded again, it was destroyed by ruling nations but thankfully with learning by rote, each generation taught their children, so it was not lost.

Ezra the great Law maker banished our ancestors after the Exile, but we have to thank him for having the insight to gather all the history together again and make a written record".

"Yes my father, he was a very adept scribe, but I wonder whether he would have agreed to allowing his scriptures to be translated into Greek" said Joiada.

The King gave a little chuckle and replied,

"I'm sure he would have turned in his grave at the thoughts of it, but it brings me back to the point I was about to make", he hesitated for a moment then followed with,

"Our Lord God must have allowed it to happen or it would not have happened".

"Quite right my father, the way Hellenism has changed the other Nations since Greek Rule, I feel it has brought a freedom to our way of life" agreed Joiada.

Nathan looked at his son proudly and said,

"The Jewish Nation went astray and were taken into Exile for punishment, since we were allowed our freedom again we have once again become a worthy Nation, although we are dispersed around the known world, we have become a respected people again, I believe that our Lord God will send a Messiah not just for the Jews but for all mankind".

Joiada and his Royal friends had not expected a statement from such an eminent King as Nathan.

They all sat looking at him in amazement.

Silence reigned for what seemed like an eternity.

Meres, as usual in his quiet voice was the first to speak,

"Your Majesty, what a wonderful exclamation, if God's Own Son is sent to live with us, then your statement must be correct, we shall all be honoured by the Lord God".

"What a privilege that we will all be included" added Ashpenaz, Kedar nodded in agreement.

The King was becoming more thrilled by the minute as the conversation went on.

After a pause he commented,

"If you are the only ones who have seen the new stars and the event will be at Bethlehem", another pause then,

"You were in the right place at the right time to be able to follow the whole event through, you have been really blessed".

Joiada looked at his friends and added,

"That must have been why Shadrach sent us, God's hand was there when Kedar first saw it".

"And Uncle Shadrach realised, Joiada told us of the Scriptures and you agreed my Lord King and I feel so privileged " Ashpenaz blurted out with excitement.

Each one of them was so exhilarated the way everything had now come together, King Nathan raised his hands gently and smiled as he calmly said,

"My children, I hope with all my heart that at last the Messiah is about to appear, but we must keep our heads and try to take it in our stride, or I should say, in your stride because you are the ones to follow, I feel so proud that I may have witnessed your part in it".

The tingling was still there, but Nathan's words had the calming influence he had desired, they felt ecstatic.

Nathan followed with something that had a much more calming effect as he reminded them,

"Have you given a thought about Herod"?

Indeed, the name of Herod drained all excitement away. Joiada said,

"Oh yes my father, I have told them about Herod".

"Yes my son, but don't feel too daunted, if our Lord God indeed has it in hand, you need not fear King Herod, he may be a tyrant but he wont stop the Son of God coming to live with us if it is His Will".

Nathan's words rang out like a bell, they felt very reassured that their quest was indestructible, nothing in the world would hold them back from the assignment they had been commissioned with.

The King dismissed them for the night, he knew they were floating on high, he could feel it himself, each one of them riding on cloud nine.

Joiada and his friends had an early call to observe the stars for an hour before dawn.

Unfortunately they did not have a very good session.

The month was Tishrei, (October) the Jewish New year festival. It was also the month when the autumn rains began, clouds were making it difficult for them to observe, the sky was only clear for a few minutes at a time.

They did however manage to take a bearing long enough for them to plot the position of Triune.

The three stars were now very much closer together, this combined with them appearing larger added considerably to the brightness of the cluster.

" Kedar, the movement is still constant, don't you think"? asked Meres.

"I feel positive it is" replied Kedar, "Do you agree Ashpenaz"?

Ashpenaz nodded as he waited for a wisp of cloud to clear his vision, then he looked at them and added,

"It's still on track to conjoin with Spica".

Joiada thought about it for a moment and said,

"My, if they do converge it will be nearly as bright as the moon".

"If we need to be in the Bethlehem area when they fall, we have to work out travelling time and distance" Meres declared.

All of a sudden, time became an important factor in their planning.

Up to now they had been able to amble almost, study and plot, research the scriptures, all at a leisurely pace.

But suddenly, in order to complete their task, they had to be in a certain place at a certain time before Triune disappeared over the horizon of the night sky.

King Nathan was ready and waiting to hear the latest news about Triune, as they greeted him with the usual protocol, he sensed they were a little agitated about their findings.

"Come my young Princes, I have the feeling you are a little tense about something, please tell me all about it" invited the King.

Joiada told his father how abruptly they realised their quest hinged upon many factors.

The King listened with great interest as first one and then the other told of their uncertainties that had cropped up.

After a few minutes the wise old King smiled at them and said,

"Last night we were all so much on a high, I'm not surprised that all of a sudden you realise the vast importance of such a responsibility.

If we are assuming that all this is an assignment that our Lord God has set you, it is understandable that the enormity of it suddenly seems to be a daunting prospect".

They each sat and thought about it.

Nathan's words slowly penetrated their minds. One by one a look of relief showed on their faces.

Meres looked at the King and said,

"Thank you your Majesty, you are so right, last night you spoke of God being in charge, if we have been chosen then it will happen, if not, it won't".

"How true my young Prince, that is how you must treat the whole project.

If you Princes are destined to herald the Son of God, nothing will come along to impede your progress and you will be there soon enough".

"Even though we may have some cloud from now on" Ashpenaz quipped with a grin on his face.

"You will have to overcome more than a bit of cloud, you will need to see Herod" replied the King.

Joiada looked at his father, frowned but slowly he started to smile.

Everyone knew what a terrible, treacherous man he was.

"We need to sort out now just how we are going to deal with going through Herod's territory, we keep mentioning his name so we'll get it sorted now", said Joiada as he smiled at his father.

The King smiled back and replied,

"The sooner you decide how you are going to deal with it, you will not worry about it again, then it wont obstruct your planning of the more vital aspects of your quest".

"We could do with you coming with us my Lord King, you

would be a great asset" remarked Ashpenaz.

The other Princes agreed.

"How do you think we should approach him father"? asked Joiada.

"Protocol must be observed, if you go and ask his advice about it, I'm sure he will give you permission to make enquiries".

"Just what do we need to enquire about my Lord King"? asked Kedar.

"Oh I'm so thrilled to be part of this"

replied King Nathan, and followed with,

"All the Prophecies point to a Saviour coming to live with us, it mentions a Virgin giving birth to a Baby, according to another prophecy it will take place in Bethlehem".

"We must definitely follow the route to Bethlehem then" Joiada remarked.

"I'm sure that will be where it will take place, it was always known as David's Town, that's where the Great King David was born, it all adds up to being there", replied Nathan, then added,

"Isa 9,7 says,

'He will reign on David's Throne".

"I think you have a good reason to let Herod know you have seen a very unusual happening in the stars that could point to the Messiah. The Jews have let all people know of their expectations of a Great Leader to be sent by the Lord God and you are sure that this is the sign of a new King"

"You are sure my Lord King that he will know about it" inquired Kedar.

"He will ask his advisors if he doesn't, they will know all the answers for you, I am hoping that it will make him feel important and pleased you asked his advice", said the King.

"Ah" retorted Ashpenaz, "Get on the right side of him from the beginning".

"Perhaps keep it to ourselves that we know about Bethlehem"? Joiada remarked.

King Nathan thought a moment and replied,

"Yes, you have interpreted the sign to be the birth of a new King which could be the King of the Jews". He lifted a finger in the air to emphasise the importance of the fact.

"You had reservations about meeting Herod yourself, have you changed your mind Joiada"? Meres asked.

King Nathan looked at his son quizzically and said,

"You still haven't forgiven him about the Synagogue have you my son" then he added

"I'm sure he won't recognise you".

"I'll keep in the background while Kedar, Meres and Ashpenaz seek an audience" replied Joiada.

"Mmmm" mumbled the King quietly, then his face brightened up and he said,

"We are Samaritan Jews, if you three non-Jewish Princes from different regions, each of you belonging to the League of International Astronomers bring to his attention of a new unusual star cluster, it will add more significance to your visit".

"Brilliant my Lord King" said Ashpenaz, "I could mention Uncle Shadrach's advice to us about following the star cluster from Babylon".

"Wow" exclaimed Kedar, "King Shadrach is known everywhere for his Astronomical studies".

"You have a point Kedar, but *You* must take credit for finding it, don't be modest"

King Nathan was very adamant as he pointed to Kedar.

The others agreed and made sure they would see to it that Kedar's name would be mentioned.

Suddenly Joiada thought of their conversation after studying the morning stars before dawn.

"I'm so glad we have worked out the time that Triune will fall out of sight" he reminded them.

"Yes" replied Meres, "We must concentrate on working out the rest of our route according to the time left, especially to allow time to see Herod".

"That sounds as though you will soon be leaving again".

King Nathan sounded quite sad at the thought and added,

"I've so enjoyed your presence with me, I have been uplifted more than I would have dreamed possible in my old age, it is many years since I have felt so important".

"We will keep you informed by messenger my father, I know you will be anxious to know how it all turns out", then Joiada added,

"You have been a great help with your wise advice".

Joiada held his father's hand, they had always been very close.

"I've noticed you call the stars 'Triune'" remarked the King.

"Kedar suggested the name, he did not want it called Kedar" replied Joiada.

"You are very modest Kedar" then after a thoughtful pause Nathan followed with, "But that name really suits the three special stars".

The King knew they had important decisions to make about their assignment without his hindrance.

He withdrew and left them to work out the rest of their Journey.

The direction of Bethlehem was southwest more or less towards Damascus.

This was where Joiada's family had built their first Caravansary.

So that was the obvious choice for them to continue their Journey.

From there they would have to change course altogether to take them south toward Bethlehem.

Since they first saw the star they had been travelling for five months and were well in front of Triune, it would be a month before it reached Palmyra.

The time of Triune's fall would be a little over three months, Bethlehem would be a months steady travel. This gave ample time for them to make any calls, and more importantly make early morning and evening observations to follow Triune's progress.

The Feast of Tabernacles.

The next day was The Feast of Tabernacles, so called from the time that the Hebrews left Egypt and lived in the desert.

Temporary shelters were built as they travelled about from place to place and Moses told them they must celebrate this every year to remind them of living in the desert.

It was one of the most important Festivals of their year, this gave King Nathan plenty of organising to do.

All desert people are known for their hospitality. Any strangers are given a meal any time of the year, they are given the title of, 'a guest of God'.

On this day during such a Special Feast, all visitors are welcome to eat anything on offer, which included a veritable banquet.

Preparations had been under way for two weeks making sure there would be plenty of food and entertainment for the day.

The whole staff had been excitedly working since well before dawn preparing enough for the whole day.

For the past week rough shelters, or booths had been erected outside the Caravansary all around the orchards and cattle sheds.

Benches for seats and tables had also been set out.

Kedar, Meres and Ashpenaz had wondered what all the staff had been doing outside most of the time since their arrival but with being so engrossed in their assignment they had not asked for an explanation.

Local farmers with their families had appeared as if from nowhere to lend a helping hand.

Food, wine and barley beer would be available for whoever came along, any work done today would be enjoyable, like a working holiday.

By the time the three Royal Princes greeted Joiada they looked at him quizzically, already the smell of cooking had filled the air for well over an hour, yet it was only the first hour of the day. (7 am)

An ox roast was part of the Festival, it had been roasting long enough to make everyone hungry.

"You didn't say anything last night about a Feast, did you"? asked Ashpenaz, still looking at Joiada as he grinned and said,

"I hope whatever it is we can join in".

Joiada answered with that great big smile on his face,

"I almost forgot myself, but when I noticed the activity three days ago I thought it would be a nice surprise for the three of you".

"Are the animals sacrificed" asked Meres.

"Some have been chosen for family and friends attending the Synagogue Service of Thanksgiving, but all are welcome to join in the festivities and eat their fill regardless".

"You must be expecting a great deal of people, perhaps from miles around"? asked Kedar.

Joiada chuckled before he answered,

"Some would have travelled most of yesterday, they make it an annual holiday, as they arrive they are given refreshments if they have come long distances".

"What if Herod came" grinned Ashpenaz.

"He would also be a guest of God" replied Joiada.

It was noticeable that they had not seen His Majesty King Nathan, usually by this time each morning he had been along to greet them.

"May I assume His Majesty is involved somewhere amongst all the preparations" Meres remarked.

"It depends where he happens to be at the time of the Festival, but the one thing he loves to take part in every year, is get involved roasting the ox.

Once the fire is alight and he is satisfied that everything is satisfactory, he will go around and mingle with anyone and everyone to encourage all the staff to enjoy the holiday", replied Joiada.

The three Princes were aware of Jewish Festivals but they had never realised just how involved with local people it could be.

Meres was prompted to comment,

"I understood these festivals were for the Jews only".

"As you know, we Samaritans are not as strict, some Jews would never condescend to mix with other nationalities, but we were told from the beginning that we must entertain the alien and the stranger, we have decided to invite them", replied Joiada, then he added,

"Go see for yourselves and enjoy".

When the three friends did see for themselves, they could not believe such a transformation could have taken place in such a short time.

The Synagogue was about a quarter of a mile from the Caravan Complex.

It had been built by the family over a hundred years previous but was used by anyone wishing to attend.

When the Israelites were taken into Exile they had to change the style of worship because their Temple had been destroyed.

To begin with they met in turn in their houses in order to worship God. Eventually synagogues were built for meetings and worship, where ten or more male Jews could gather, they could start a new synagogue of their own.

Like all large cities there were more than one synagogue.

The word synagogue is Greek for 'meeting', it has a similar meaning to 'church', it does not actually refer to the building, but the people gathered inside.

Two areas were set apart for displays of dancing or singing groups with musicians to perform throughout the day. Local people could get up and dance themselves if organised groups were not 'on stage'.

One little band had already invited some locals to begin the merriment.

There was even a travelling circus group, limbering up for later.

Along the pathways were stalls with drinks and all manner of light refreshments on offer.

Several stalls had sweet delicacies that enticed children to make queues.

"There are a quite a few sweet toothed adults in those queues" said Ashpenaz.

"Knowing you" replied Kedar, "You will be one of them soon".

"Oh to be young again" quipped Meres.

"Did Joiada say why he didn't join us"? asked Kedar.

"He's taking part in the synagogue Service of Thanksgiving later today", replied Meres, then added, "I wonder if I could attend".

"I would like to attend myself" said Ashpenaz.

"I'll ask if we would be allowed to perhaps sit in the back ground" Kedar added.

When they met Joiada an hour later he was supervising the layout of a large group of tables set out under the trees that could seat a hundred people or more, this particular area was for family and invited friends.

When Joiada saw them coming towards him he shouted,

"There you are my Royal Comrades, what do you think of our celebrations so far"?

"I've heard of your Feasts but never guessed that they could be on such a grand scale as we've seen, how many do you think will turn up" asked Kedar.

"Haven't got a clue" was the modest reply, "The idea is to give a treat to anyone wishing to come and join in thanking our Great God for all he has given us during the year".

"Any stranger can mingle and eat as he wishes"? Ashpenaz inquired.

"The more the merrier" was the reply, "Everything is free, lots of produce is brought and given by the locals who run the sucs, (market stalls) it officially begins on the fourth hour with a procession led by the band".

Meres put his hand up to shade the sun, from its position he said,

"That will be in about half an hour then"?

"Those taking part have been forming the parade since the third hour" stated Joiada and he grinned at the look of wonder on his friend's faces.

Meres asked almost with a note of begging in his quiet voice,

"Joiada, do you mind if we attend the Service at your Synagogue"?

Joiada looked at them so seriously, Meres wondered if he had overstepped the bond of friendship.

Joiada looked at them, paused and said,

"What, the three of you".

Meres was wishing he had not made such a request.

He said, "We did not wish to offend".

Joiada suddenly burst out laughing, he could not restrain himself any longer.

He got hold of their hands one by one and said,

"When I tell the King of your request he will be overjoyed, he wanted to invite you but he also did not wish you to be offended, it's not everyone who wishes to worship with us" then he added,

"You've made my day".

Once again their bond had become stronger.

Suddenly they heard the sound of drums, it was the forth hour.

Joiada exclaimed excitedly,

"Come quickly to join the King".

He rushed off with them in close pursuit to a rostrum that had been erected near the gateway of the Caravansary.

Within minutes they had climbed up and were standing by King Nathan with other dignitaries.

The drums slowly became louder until they appeared about two hundred yards to their left.

Leading them were two camels with riders who had been bedecked with the Royal Family Colours.

The parade was led by a Herald carrying the Royal Banner.

The King himself was dressed in dazzling white, his silk turban aglow with precious stones was quite impressive as it caught the morning sunshine, all adding to the regal splendour of his appearance.

When the Herald was fifty yards away from the King, trumpets began to play in time with the drums.

As the fanfare ended they were almost level with the King, other instruments began to play, and like all marching bands the crowds of people that had gathered began to clap in rhythm adding to the spectacle as the parade processed by.

His Majesty held his hand over them as they passed, to give them his blessing.

The band was made up of drums, trumpets, a mixture of other instruments, woodwind and percussion, making about fifty in all.

Behind them came dancers bedecked with streamers, male and

female, they also had tambourines to tap to the tempo of the music.

It was indeed a Carnival to celebrate the occasion of bringing in the harvest.

Carts pulled by many different animals had been decorated and loaded with all manner of fruit and vegetables.

Great clusters of grapes, figs and dates brought up the rear.

Most of the produce had been brought by the more well to do farmers to distribute to the poor at the end of the day, none of whom went home empty handed.

Tradition was that the grapes were being taken to vats where locals enjoyed a session of wine treading, this was all part and partial of the proceedings.

It was almost an hour before the whole parade had passed by.

The Royal guests had experienced similar events before but this one had somehow touched them in a different way. They could not explain just why it seemed so different, this was a procedure that took place when the harvest was brought home in most countries, Meres was prompted to say,

"Do you think that since we followed Triune we are more aware how important it is to thank God for His goodness".

As soon as he had said it he felt a little self-conscious, he looked down wondering what the others might say.

"I thought it was just me" replied Ashpenaz.

"That means it has made the three of us realise that we are now looking at life entirely in a new way" Kedar exclaimed.

Joiada had heard them, he said, "I'm convinced you will be even more moved after the Thanksgiving Service".

The Service was to be held at the eighth hour, (2 pm) Joiada said he would meet them outside the Synagogue a quarter hour before and told them to enjoy whatever was on offer until then.

The array of food was very varied, every taste had been catered for except for anyone wanting pork.

Roast ducks, a calf, all types of fowled birds, lambs and kids, were on offer.

All cut into small pieces and served on large leaves of various plants.

Meat and vegetable stews were served in small earthenware dishes, with salads.

Several types of cheese made from the milk of camels, cows, goats and sheep were served with small loaves of bread and cakes of dried fruit.

The three friends were amazed. What they really found hard to believe was the fact that it was all free for anyone and everyone, they knew the poor were helped almost everywhere but never before had they witnessed it on such a huge scale.

Rich and poor mingled and rubbed shoulders together, something that very rarely happened at any other time.

It was truly a great experience, their royalty usually placed them in great respect but today they were just one of the crowd, and they were really enjoying it.

After sampling many of the delicacies on offer together with the varied entertainment they suddenly realised it was time to meet Joiada at the Synagogue.

As they neared the area they saw a crowd had gathered at the side of the building around a large piece of natural stone, the flat top of it was quite blood stained.

Joiada and his father were standing among a small group of personnel, very close to the stone.

With them was a tall figure dressed in a splendid outfit of many colours.

The mitre on his head alone made him so resplendent, but as they came closer there were many other spectacular features about his dress that made him more impressive.

On the upper part of his body he wore an apron that had four rows of large precious stones, three in each row.

Joiada saw them coming and beckoned them to join him.

This placed them at the front of the proceedings taking place outside the Synagogue.

To us, in this day and age, it would be quite gruesome, but the way of life in those days was what we would call the 'norm'.

A dozen or so animals, lambs and goats were being slaughtered one by one for the ritual festivity sacrifices.

It was an honour to be present while the High Priest blessed each animal before it was killed, the person richly attired, was the High Priest performing this duty.

The three Royal Guests took it in their stride, this was the way of life to them, the great difference was that these animals had been specially chosen for the occasion. They may even have been bred for the purpose.

Joiada could see that they were a little perplexed to witness such a procedure. After a few minutes he took them aside to explain what was taking place.

"You must be wondering just why we seem to be butchering animals so close to our place of worship"? he explained after they had moved away.

Meres as usual had some sort of answer,

"I know that many animals are sacrificed in the Temple Grounds in Jerusalem, I imagine it is similar" he said.

Joiada answered as he nodded to affirm it.

"You will join us at the large area you saw being set out for tonight, there will be around a hundred guests, these animals will be roasted along with wild fowl, roast duck and numerous other game".

"I can't wait" retorted Ashpenaz, then added, "Who's the one all dressed up"?

Joiada and the others burst out laughing, Kedar said,

"Trust you to let us down Ashpenaz".

Joiada followed with,

"Well he always did speak his mind", then he explained.

"The man all dressed up is our High Priest, he commits each animal to God before it dies, it all goes back in tradition to when animals were burnt as a sacrifice to God for his goodness, over the many years we have changed the procedure to what you a witnessing".

"The dress of the High Priest, has it always been the same"? asked Meres.

"Yes, God gave the instructions to Moses Himself just what he should wear" Joiada explained.

"What are the twelve precious stones for"? asked Ashpenaz.

"Originally there were twelve Tribes of Israel, God even gave orders what the gems should be" Joiada explained.

"I noticed a gold plate fastened to his mitre with something written on it", Kedar said,

"Is that something important".

Joiada nodded his head, he looked very serious now, even Ashpenaz waited with baited breath just to hear what it was.

"On that gold plate is the NAME of Our Lord God, we do not speak it, but it is spelt like this".

Joiada took out of a little container a small piece of parchment, on which was written the letters 'YHWY.

When they had seen the way it was spelt Meres said,

"No one could pronounce that, that must be just why the letters are so arranged".

"When Moses was sent to ask Pharaoh to let his people go, Moses asked God,

'Who shall I say has sent me if I am asked'?

"God said "Tell Pharoah, 'I AM, WHO I AM' has sent you. We say it is,

'HE IS, WHO HE IS', but we always avoid it if possible".

"I am beginning to understand just how you feel about Your God" said Meres.

"Our God" said Kedar.

"And mine" remarked Ashpenaz, then after a pause he followed with,

"I hope He'll have me".

"I'm sure he will" said Joiada as he gently patted Ashpenaz on his shoulder.

As the sacrificing came to and end, they began to move into the Synagogue.

Before Joiada had left them earlier he told them to have their Magi Turbans with them to wear during the Service.

The turbans are a special dark blue silk in contrast to show the 'Gold Time Star' as if it was in the dark starlit sky.

The Time Star had twelve points, hours of the day.

It was worn by Members of the Magi League, after they had proved themselves worthy.

The Gold Time Star with the name of the Magi engraved upon it, was presented when they Graduated from the Academy.

These special turbans were recognised as the Magi Symbol all over the known world.

The guests were ushered into seats near the front with Joiada leading them in.

Four Magi together was quite an unusual sight among the regular Synagogue worshippers.

An area with special seating was front centre facing the congregation.

All the seats were taken except one in the middle of the front row.

The King entered and took this seat.

A robed figure entered carrying an incense burner, making his way to the front and placed it on a metal holder, slowly the incense filled the building with a strong aroma that was slightly acrid.

As soon as the King was seated, from another entrance a choir began to sing psalm 67, 'May God be gracious to us', a thanksgiving psalm praising God for the harvest.

The congregation stood up while the choir processed to their place as they sang.

Two other robed attendants followed, with the High Priest following behind them.

The choir remained standing as they reached their seats, the High Priest stood in front of a very elaborate high chair raised on a dais.

When the choir had finished singing, he climbed up to take his seat, the congregation now sat down.

A very impressive service followed, prayers were offered for the bountiful harvest, after another psalm was sung, one of the other priests walked to a flight of steps that led up to a niche in the wall.

After climbing the steps he reached into the aperture and took out a large scroll.

This was the Torah, the Holy Scriptures, he descended and

carried them towards the High Priest and placed them on a lectern near the altar.

After turning the scroll he began to read:

Be Joyful at your feast, you, your sons and daughters,
Your menservants and maidservants,
And the widows who live in your towns.
(V17) Each of you must bring a gift in proportion to the way
the Lord Your God has blessed you. Deut 16, 14-17

At the end of the Service a large container had been placed near the door for donations to the poor and needy.

The three Princes gave generously and were thanked by the stewards.

Outside Joiada asked them what they thought about the experience.

"I have always found it very odd that people in various lands worship such strange deities", said Meres, "Your worship of a Deity who has created the heavens and the earth and supplied us with all our bounty has much more meaning to it".

"Yes" exclaimed Ashpenaz, "Names like 'Diana the huntress' or 'Hermes the messenger', seem very vague when you compare them with God who created everything seen and unseen".

"I can only say that Our God is Awesome" added Kedar.

King Nathan was now near enough for him to overhear Kedar.

"How wonderful to hear you say that Kedar, you said OUR GOD.

That proves you are ready to go and welcome His Son".

The King put his hand on Kedar's shoulder,

"I feel I should mention you to the High Priest, if the three of you are of the same mind he will welcome you as Proselytes".

When Gentiles wished to worship The God of Abraham, they became Proselytes.

Obviously, when the High Priest was told he held a little ceremony in the Synagogue, because of who they were, he felt very privileged.

The temperature was much more tolerable now half way through the month of Tishrea, (October) 20-25 degrees centigrade

As the special guests arrived for the feast many of the other visitors wished to talk with the Magi.

Some had wondered whether there may be something special that had prompted them to visit.

Joiada, however, told them that they had studied together at the Academy of Astronomy at Alexandria, they accepted it was just a reunion.

One or two did tentatively ask if they had seen anything unusual in the stars.

The animals sacrificed earlier were now ready.

The air was filled with a wonderful aroma of all the roast meats soon to be served.

King Nathan was there to greet the guests as they arrived, servants showed them to their seats.

Drinks were served while they waited, soft music played in the background.

Joiada and his friends sat together, on this occasion they were dressed like Royal Princes, the Magi turbans made their appearance very regal.

The High Priest arrived and was led to where two special seats had been arranged.

He sat down and was soon joined by King Nathan.

Before the King sat down he held up his hand and very quickly all talking ceased.

"What a wonderful day" the King stated, he paused and looked round at all his guests, it was obvious he was very pleased with how everything had unfolded right from the beginning of the celebrations, he continued, "Our Lord God has blessed us with a bountiful harvest, loyal friends, a loving family, our very eminent High Priest" the King held his hand out to him who also acknowledged the greeting.

The High Priest stood and replied,

"Your Majesty, we thank the Lord God for all you do for us", spontaneous clapping broke out, the High Priest paused for a moment then continued, "His Majesty has asked me to bless the food we have", he raised his hand and his eyes upward towards heaven and pronounced a short prayer of thanks for such bountiful provisions.

The Celebratory Feast began and continued late into the night, the guests enjoyed the King's hospitality to the full, quite a few of them had to be helped on their way a few hours later but this was all part and parcel of this annual festival.

Joiada's three Royal Magi had enjoyed this new experience, the respect they had received, the whole atmosphere of spending so much time with people who worshipped the God of Abraham had allowed them to see a brand new way of life, a life that appealed to an unknown part of their being. Something so different they could not explain it.

The feast had been laid outside under the trees, there had been a few clouds in the sky but otherwise it was favourable for observation.

Joiada noticed how his friends were looking up to the heavens and sent word to Eli. A message came back almost immediately that all had been set up.

"Eli had anticipated our thoughts, everything it set up ready".

Their attendants came to take their turbans and cloaks and replaced them with suitable attire for them to go climbing the observation tower.

Less than half an hour later they were in their elements to see the latest position of Triune.

"I think we can safely say it has left the Constellation of Leo and joined Virgo" Meres exclaimed.

"It is definitely on track to join Spica" Ashpenaz said.

Joiada thought about it for a moment and said, "How about arranging to continue our Journey tomorrow to Damascus".

"I'm all for that, we must stay ahead while we can" said Ashpenaz, "Circumstances may arise putting us in the wrong place".

"Yes, we must take every opportunity to keep ahead" added Kedar.

The Festival of Tabernacles was held during the full moon, this indeed gave the night sky that extra luminescence they had enjoyed so many times together from the time when they had studied as students.

Since Triune had appeared to lead them on this adventure of a lifetime, it was almost as if they were on automatic pilot.

A few moments later they were aware of another person joining them.

"Father" Joiada shouted, "What a lovely surprise, you have come to share this moment with us".

"I wondered if I dare hope to perhaps see even for a second just what you are witnessing".

The King was almost pleading for them to let him try.

The four princes all offered their position and instruments for the King to see for himself.

"I'll use Kedar's dioptra" the King commented, "It was his apparatus that found it".

Kedar helped Nathan to take the stance in order to look through the tubes each end.

"Make yourself comfortable your Majesty" said Kedar, "place your best eye almost on the tube, don't strain, close the other eye and just focus gently".

Quite a few moments went by, they were all wondering if he would be able to adjust enough to let him have at least a glance.

Suddenly he shouted almost at the top of his voice,

"Oh, thank you My Lord God, thank you".

Joiada, Kedar and Meres all looked up without their instruments, at that precise moment a shooting star dropped from Triune, half way down the night sky.

"Did you see that"? asked Kedar.

"We did" replied Ashpenaz and Meres.

"I saw everything" King Nathan exclaimed, "Just before my eyes watered, I was able to make out the three stars, and I'm sure that shooting star was just for me".

The others were amazed that Nathan mentioned it, it proved that just for a moment he had been able to focus on Triune.

Nathan was elated.

"I've seen the heralding of The Messiah" he said slowly and emphatically.

Joiada was so pleased that his father had been able to experience even for a split second what had brought them together in this moment of time.

Even in the moonlight they could tell that the King was in the seventh heaven.

As he made his way to climb down the steps Joiada and Meres automatically helped him down.

After they had descended and made their way in doors the King was glad to sit down, the experience had left him somewhat overwhelmed.

Joiada saw his father to his bed and joined them in the usual room to discuss what they had seen.

"Is his majesty well" asked Ashpenaz.

The others also waited for a reply.

Joiada smiled as he said, "He assured me he was fine, he kept saying over and over again, 'I have seen it".

"He was truly overcome by the experience, but just when that shooting star dropped at that precise second it was unbelievable" said Kedar.

"King Nathan does love his God, I'm sure he was meant to see even if it was only for a second that spectacular moment in time" remarked Meres.

"Do you have the feeling we should be on our way"? Joiada asked them.

"It's every time we see it, we all have the same feeling" answered Ashpenaz, and followed with,

"I could go and jump on my camel right now".

They were all so eager, they decided to spend the following day preparing, and leave for Damascus two hours before sundown.

Despite King Nathan's extraordinary witnessing of such a spectacular sign, he was up and about like a two year old helping the Princes to get their gear together for the next leg of their Journey.

Although family and friends were aware of the star gazing episodes they had not been informed of how important it could be.

For the time being King Nathan thought it best to wait a little longer before telling the family.

When they were almost ready to leave, the King gathered them together in their little study room, he wanted to see them for a special reason.

He sat waiting for them and bade them to sit for a moment.

"Joiada my son, bring the Princes in, I wish to give my Blessing before you go".

Joiada sat beside him while the others quietly sat closeby, they felt very moved as they gathered round the King.

Before Nathan spoke he unwrapped a small box and handed it to Joiada.

"Please take this for me and give it to the Holy Child when you see Him".

Joiada was dumbfounded, he took the box and held it up for all to see.

"I visited a warehouse of ours two months ago and some Princes from Arabia had come to do business with us, at the end of our transactions one of them gave me this gift" said Nathan as he sat looking at them.

He continued, "The Prince assured me that it contained some of the finest quality Frankincense that could be obtained, I heard you mention that you were taking some as a gift, please take that for me".

Nathan now had tears rolling down his cheeks as he reached for a silk kerchief to dry his eyes.

"We will convey this gift and make sure it is given to The Messiah" replied Joiada.

He stood up and lifted his hand to them, "Our God moves in a mysterious way" the King declared.

They all had watery eyes.

After Nathan had composed himself he addressed them.

Please give my love to your lovely wife Princess Ruth, Simeon my son, Matred and Doris my daughters, and tell Queen Mother

Sarah, her King still loves her and I hope to see her soon".

The King had gained his composure now.

"May the Blessing of the Lord God go with you as you Journey to see His Son".

He put protocol aside for the next few moments as he took them one by one and hugged them.

Obviously his son had an extra hug.

The whole staff had appeared to see them on their way, they did not know just what was so special about this occasion but they had a suspicion that it was indeed something very extraordinary.

Even the visiting business clients showed respect and stood still as they processed out of the Caravansary.

And so the four Princes once again continued on their way to follow the Star Cluster they had named Triune.

Two hours later after the sun had set, they made camp almost eighteen miles nearer their quest.

A few clouds were around but the sky was clear enough for their servants to set up the gear used while travelling.

While a light supper was prepared they observed the progress of Triune.

It was now very noticeable how bright the three stars were and how much closer together they were.

Out in the countryside there was no light pollution, this gave extra brightness to the night sky.

"It is going to join with Spica unless it passes on by" exclaimed Meres, he moved over for Ashpenaz to take a look.

"It has followed almost a straight line, all three stars are as bright as Danebola" Ashpenaz said.

"Move over, you keep telling me it's my star, now I can't get a look in" shouted Kedar with a chuckle.

"I knew you would want to hog it when you'd got over finding it".

Said Joiada, gently pushing Kedar out of the way.

One of Joiada's older servants who had known his master since he was a teenager was close by, he jokingly said,

"I hope I haven't got to fetch the King to my young Prince".

The others pointed a finger at Joiada,

Ashpenaz quipped,

"I'm glad someone is here to keep you in order".

Joiada looked at his servant, he was grinning as he said,

"If you haven't got my supper ready in two minutes I shall send you home".

The older servant went off to the camp-fire laughing all the way.

A rumble in the distance was heard and they all shouted, "Rain".

Two tents were erected within half an hour one for the princes, one for their staff. The animals were settled for the night, a fire had been lit, the tent openings both faced the fire so by the time the rain had started they were all undercover having their supper.

"We've been very fortunate to have come from Babylon in good weather, although some days it was very hot" remarked Kedar.

"Yes, now the autumn rains have begun we will have to study the stars when we can", said Joiada.

"If we have to visit Herod, that's the least of our worries" said Ashpenaz.

"If Our God is with us, Herod won't stand a chance" added Meres.

They each rolled back on their makeshift mattresses laughing.

Soon they were fast asleep regardless of the thunder and lightning around them.

Indeed the best of the weather now proved to be behind them.

They needed the tents for the next five nights as they travelled and camped during the one hundred and fifty miles to their next destination.

Damascus

Saints, before the altar bending, watching long in hope and fear,
Suddenly the Lord descending, in His temple shall appear.
(J Montgomery)

Damascus was one of the oldest continually inhabited Cities in the world.

The Barada River had a system of canals and tunnels that maximised the irrigation to the areas that were fertile.

As the traveller approached it, it looked like a green oasis port in the desert.

Since the time of Solomon it was known as a Royal City. It had been a stronghold for many kings.

Situated at the foot of the Lebanon Hills from which small streams ran through the thronged streets.

Trade Routes converged from Aleppo in the north, eastwards to Indo-China and south to Egypt and Petra.

Picturesque markets stocked by Caravans from before the time of Abraham, sold goods from all the known countries, the variety of which could not be excelled.

It would be near here, on the road from Jerusalem perhaps forty five years later, that St. Paul would have his vision of a blinding light.

Later he would escape from the Jews after his conversion, by being lowered in a basket from the City Wall.

Although it was Hellenised, it had a large population of nomads.

It was famous for it's silk markets and of course Damascus Steel, of which it was said to be hardened through a process involving camel dung.

The fertile fields around produced not only great quantities of fruit and vegetables but outstanding vintage wine.

It was about the sixth hour, (noon) as Joiada led them almost to enter the city, then he turned onto the northern route, his family Caravansary was half a mile out of the city on this route.

It was the oldest of their establishments, the first one the family had built, it had been here for over seventy years, built by Nathan's father.

Prior to that the family themselves had been Syndiarchs.

The little camel train of Royal Princes moved quicker than the commercial traffic, so it was easily recognised by the staff long before it entered the quadrangle.

A waiting line of attendants welcomed them as their mounts knelt for them to dismount.

A young lady in her early twenties stood at the main doorway.

As soon as Joiada had dismounted she ran and threw her arms around him.

They hugged each other for a minute or two, as she looked up at Joiada she had a tear rolling down her cheek, she said,

"At long last my father has returned".

Joiada looked down at her and softly replied,

"My Princess".

Ashpenaz looked in surprise and retorted to Meres and Kedar,

"It's Princess Rebecca".

Over the years, she had grown into a beautiful young woman, dressed in the finest of silks, but only a minimum amount of jewellery.

As his Royal friends came nearer Joiada asked,

"Do you remember Rebecca"?

She bowed as they approached, they bowed to her in response.

"How the buds do blossom, what a lovely daughter you have Joiada" Ashpenaz remarked.

"It must be ten years or more since you saw her" said Joiada as he looked at her proudly.

She smiled and said,

"Please come this way my Royal Guests, we knew you would be here soon, your rooms are waiting for you".

Again they were to enjoy the hospitality of Joiada's family. Each member of the Royal Party had their mounts and pack animals taken to give them refreshing food or fodder as the case may be, it was most welcome after their spell of camping each night.

Joiada saw his friends in and was about to enter when a voice shouted,

"Prince Jo from Samaria".

Joiada turned and looked, as he recognised the owner of the voice he replied,

"Prince Jo from Jerusalem".

One of the merchants came up to Joiada and they greeted each other.

His name was Josiah, he was a Jew from a village outside Jerusalem, business had brought them together fifteen years ago and they had become very firm and well respected friends.

They both used the short term "Jo" for each other, it had become,

Jo from Jerusalem, and Jo from Samaria.

"Are you alone" asked Joiada.

"Yes, other than my servants, I have to be in Aleppo in a few days, I shall just stay here over night".

"Please join me later for lunch and I'll introduce you to my friends, they were with me at the Academy of Astronomy".

"You are so kind my Royal friend, I would be honoured to do so" he replied.

Two hours later Joiada sat with his friends and told them about Josiah from Jerusalem.

He had sent a messenger to bring him to join them for their meal that had been set up in the cloisters.

"Do you have many Jewish friends from Jerusalem"? Kedar asked.

"One or two business acquaintances, but Josiah is so different, he loves to mix with other people, I don't know any other Judean Jews so liberal as Josiah".

"How do his own people take him, do they reproach him at all" Ashpenaz asked.

"I don't think it would bother him, he genuinely likes to talk to anyone" replied Joiada.

They saw their guest being led by the messenger and they all rose to greet him.

After the greetings were over they sat to enjoy a refreshing drink before the meal was served.

"My friends are on their way to becoming Proselytes" Joiada told his Jewish friend.

Josiah looked at each one and replied,

"How wonderful, may I ask if anything particular has helped to make you believe in Our Lord God"?

Joiada was not quite ready for that question, he looked at his three friends and tentatively answered,

"An incident has arisen whereby they wanted to study our Scriptures, they have become quite absorbed in their research, they joined my father and me at our Thanksgiving Service during the Feast of Tabernacles while we were at Palmyra".

This truly was something special, a look of surprise showed on his face.

"I'm so pleased for my Royal Princes, what did you think of the Jewish way of worship" asked Josiah.

"It makes much more sense than worshipping idols" Meres answered.

"I wonder whether Josiah would advise us about Herod"? exclaimed Kedar.

The others looked at Kedar in surprise, they could not believe he could have mentioned anything about their quest.

Joiada was going to ask if they wished to mention it to others, or still keep it quiet for the time being.

Kedar sat there looking quite serious, he knew he had forced the issue.

He then added,

"I suddenly had the feeling that we can trust Josiah to be discreet about it".

Josiah gathered that something very important was in the air, he looked from one to the other quizzically, then said,

"Whatever you wish to talk about Joiada, you know you can trust me not to tell another soul if you do not wish me to. If I can advise you about that tyrant Herod, I will be only too pleased to do so".

"That's it then, I'm glad you mentioned it Kedar" Joiada answered with a sigh of relief.

"My Royal friends studied with me at the Alexandria Academy as students, we became inseparable. However, the bond between us has become even stronger this past few months, something very special has come along, so special we feel that for the time being we should keep it to ourselves".

When Joiada finished talking Josiah looked very serious.

After a pause he said,

"Whatever it is, it must be out of this world by the look on your faces".

"Five months ago Kedar and Meres were studying the stars in the old part of Babylon" exclaimed Joiada.

Josiah smiled and remarked,

"If you were all at the Academy of Astronomy you must each have the 'Time Star', that makes the four of you Magi Astronomers".

"Thank you for the accolade", replied Joiada

"We are only human beings, no one is more important than the other".

Josiah suddenly interrupted and burst out,

"Has one of you seen a new star"?

"Wow" gasped Ashpenaz, "You've guessed what it is all about".

Josiah held up his hands in disbelief, the look of surprise on his face had opened his eyes very wide as he sat staring at them.

After a few moments Joiada said,

"When we told King Shadrach he immediately said, it must be heralding 'The Messiah".

Now Josiah's face was full of wonder, he quietly said,

"Thanks be to God".

But after a pause he really astounded them by saying,

"That's the second time I've been told about The Messiah".

Now it was the turn of the four Princes to be surprised.

Josiah must have somehow experienced another incident alluding to the Messiah, did he know other people who studied the stars?

"We would like you to tell us all about it if you don't mind revealing it to us" Joiada invited.

"I was in The Temple at Jerusalem just after The Passover, my son was with me, he is my secretary. We had been to make a sacrifice and as we were making our way out we saw a small crowd gathered around a couple with a Baby".

The four Princes could not believe just what Josiah had said.

"A couple with a Baby" Meres almost whispered.

"Please continue" said Joiada, he was so eager to hear what Josiah had to say.

The other Princes also begged him to continue.

They waited open mouthed.

Josiah could see how enwrapped they were about witnessing what he had observed in the Temple.

"An old lady was there telling everyone in a loud voice that the Babe was very special for the Redemption of all Jerusalem".

"An old lady" enquired Joiada, "What would an old lady have to do with the Baby"?

Josiah shrugged his shoulders and added,

"Her name was Anna, she is a Prophetess according to the Officials in the Temple, she goes in daily to worship and is very well respected".

"I never thought you could have a lady who prophesied" said Meres.

"So the people must have been taking note of what she said"? Kedar retorted.

"Yes, but one of the Officials told us to go and find an old gentleman named Simeon and listen to what he had to say" replied Josiah.

The four Princes were now spellbound, they were leaning forward on the edge of their seats.

"Please go on" prompted Ashpenaz.

"We eventually found the old man sitting in one of the cloisters, he had been in the Temple most of the day, we asked if his name was Simeon".

"Go on" Joiada prompted.

"We couldn't get over the look on his face" said Josiah, "He looked radiant, you could tell he had experienced something very special.

As we approached he replied,

'I'm Simeon, have you have come to ask me about the Holy Babe".

"Yes", I said, "I heard Anna talking to the people".

"Oh yes" he replied,

"She also recognised the Babe as Someone Very Special".

"Who *are* the couple with the Baby, I asked".

"The Babe is their son, their firstborn, they had come to dedicate Him to the Lord God according to the Law".

"All first born sons are dedicated to God according to the Law of Moses", Joiada informed the three Princes.

"How old was the Child" Joiada asked.

"The mother had waited for her purification time to be over, so He must have been at least forty days old" explained Josiah.

They did some quick calculating and suddenly Meres shouted,

"That would be a some time before Triune rose".

"I can't believe how it all adds up" said Kedar,

"It was meant for us to be meeting you today" he added looking at Josiah.

The merchant prince from Jerusalem could hardly take it in about the star sign.

"Simeon told us just what happened when he saw the couple with the Child".

"Had no one told Simeon about the couple previously" asked Joiada.

"No, but as soon as he saw the Babe, he said 'The Spirit,'

revealed to him that it was God's Own Son".

"What is The Spirit" Meres asked in amazement.

"We would have come across that eventually" replied Joiada,

"But I must try and explain to you about it before we go any further".

"Please do" said Ashpenaz,

"It sounds very mysterious".

"Very briefly for the time being I'll try to bring you up to date" said Joiada,

"If we look at the very beginning of the Scriptures it explains about God creating the world. God made everything from chaos, it describes 'God's Spirit' being over the waters, it is something that cannot be seen, but it is God's hidden power".

That gave the three proselytes something to really think deeply about.

A long silent pause followed, then Meres asked,

"Could that be like lightening"?

"Close" answered Joiada, "But nothing as violent as that".

Josiah interrupted and said,

"God has often given messages to the Prophets but they have not actually seen God, He has put it into their mind as a thought, we believe it is God's Spirit at work".

"Well said" added Joiada, "A dream can be the work of the Spirit, many people recorded in the Scriptures have had dreams that conveyed messages from God".

"Like Joseph the dreamer", added Meres.

"You have taught them well Joiada, your friends are quick to learn" remarked Josiah.

Kedar exclaimed,

"When Simeon saw the Child in the Temple he realised this was The Son of God, his recognition was revealed by what you term as 'The Spirit".

Now Josiah was very impressed, he suddenly said,

"Now I understand why Magi are known as 'Wise Men', I am honoured to be in the company of such eminent men".

Meres reached out and took him by the hand and said,

"We have been very fortunate to have studied at one of the best Academies in the world, but we are only men just like you, we may have more knowledge but we are only normal people".

This helped to put Josiah at ease.

Meres asked,

"Can you remember what Simeon said when he saw The Child".

Josiah smiled at that, he began to search his pouch, he then produced a piece of papyrus and said,

"I can do better than that, this is exactly what he said. My son was with me, he is the more learned of the two of us, he is my letter writer, always handy when I'm doing business, he carries a writing kit with him so he was able to record the words of Simeon".

Josiah gave the small papyrus sheet to Joiada to read.

As we now know, these words that Simeon uttered are what we call,

The Nunc Dimitus.

Joiada read the words on the papyrus.

'Lord now lettest thou Thy servant depart in peace
For mine eyes have seen Thy salvation
And to be a light to lighten the Gentiles
And for the glory of Your people Israel'. AV Bible. Luke 2

They all sat staring at the papyrus.

With Josiah having his son trained to be his secretary, he was able to record the exact words spoken by Simeon.

Scribes, or Letter Writers, as they were called had a flat little box that contained a quill, a small container to hold water, a mixture of vegetable soot, and gum.

This mixture was devised by the Egyptians.

When the 'ink' was mixed, it was so good that thousands of papyrus sheets, pieces of pottery and other broken bits of baked clay have been found dating well over 1000 BC.

They are still quite readable.

Many can still be found in museums all over the world.

Letter writers could still be found at the roadside in cities of

Palestine during the middle of the twentieth century.

The Messiah had arrived according to what Josiah had witnessed in the Temple.

"It seems we have read the Stars correctly" said Joiada, although he was looking at Josiah. Then he followed with,

"What do you think yourself, did Anna and Simeon seem genuine".

"Most of the people in the Temple were very excited about it, the whole place was buzzing with the news" admitted Josiah.

"Was Herod about"? asked Kedar.

"He was up at Baneas overseeing a Temple dedicated to Caesar Augustus, he is going to rename the place Caesarea" answered Josiah.

They paused for thought, but were surprised when Josiah asked,

"Could I have a look at the stars with you"?

"Of course you can, we shall set up soon after sunset, I'm sure my fellow Princes won't mind at all".

"We will be able to show you what Kedar saw when it was quite tiny" remarked Ashpenaz.

"Will it be called after you Kedar"? Josiah asked.

Kedar shook his head as he replied,

"No, we are going to call it Triune".

"Why Triune"? Josiah asked again.

"There are three new stars forming a triangle" said Meres.

While they had been discussing the wonderful event witnessed by Josiah in the Temple, light refreshments were served.

At the end of their midday meal Joiada asked his friend from Jerusalem if he would join them later for the evening meal after studying the stars.

Josiah was more than pleased and said he would be honoured.

The Damascus Caravan Complex did not have a purpose built observation platform like the newer ones so their apparatus had been taken outside to a small hillock a little way from the wall.

Just before dusk the Princes made their way out with their new friend Josiah, the sun was about to disappear below the horizon.

A few clouds had gathered earlier but now the sky was quite

clear for them to study Triune.

With having to rely on the weather they were anxious to get things set up quickly in case they had to abandon it for rain.

Just two dioptras had been requested, Meres and Kedar had them both ready in minutes.

"I'm glad you can see it at this stage" said Meres "Since Kedar found it, it has become much brighter and clearer, see for yourself Josiah" invited Meres.

He gently put Josiah into the position of looking through the dioptra.

Kedar invited Ashpenaz to take his place.

Before coming out Josiah had been shown what to look for on the charts, and just where Triune was in comparison to Spica.

As soon as his eyes focused on the new stars, Josiah shouted,

"I can see the three stars, that must be Triune"?

Ashpenaz had focused now and replied,

"That is certainly Triune, it almost seems now that the whole galaxy of stars are making way for the Messiah".

"Oh my" said Josiah "I have heard two people heralding the Messiah, now I have seen a great sign in the sky, I must be the most blessed man on earth".

He moved out of the way as he invited Joiada to take his place.

"Isn't it amazing, we must have seen it most nights during the past five months and every time it looks more radiant".

"We have come a long way my dear friends" said Meres, "but I feel the time is hurrying along, I have a feeling that things will escalate now, we must be ready to travel the rest of the way at a much faster pace".

"You are so right Meres" added Joiada,

"I entirely agree, what do you say that we head south tomorrow".

"I'm ready" said Ashpenaz "I don't want to miss out on completing the mission now we've come this far".

"I'm feeling envious" Josiah admitted, "I feel sure you are to witness a very special occurrence".

Another twenty minutes was available for them to take turns

looking at Triune then the sky clouded up and they returned to their rooms just as it began to rain.

After a change of clothing they met for a lavish meal laid on once again by Joiada's Family Business.

After making arrangements for their mounts to be ready for continuing their journey the following morning, he joined them with his box of scriptures.

He decided to invite Josiah to give comments concerning the Prophets.

Another Hebrew among them could perhaps add to the education of the new Proselytes.

"Ah you've brought the scriptures Joiada, I'm sure Ashpenaz and Kedar, like me are looking forward to finding more prophecies of encouragement " remarked Meres.

"I know Josiah will be well versed in what our Prophets have written, so I hope he will point out anything he thinks is relevant" replied Joiada.

He proceeded to tell Josiah of the prophecies they had dealt with.

"I'm very impressed" said Josiah,

"I don't think there could be many more that could be applied to your quest".

"I'm sure you may add something as the evening goes by" said Joiada,

"But there is something else you could help us with if you will".

Joiada had a pleading sound in his voice, it was what he had been niggled about for days, the princes knew only too well how it had bothered him.

"I will be only too pleased to help in any way possible" replied Josiah.

"You might know what is troubling me" added Joiada,

"How are we going to deal with Herod".

Joiada had not shown how perturbed he was on the matter since they last mentioned it, but it again became obvious Herod was top most of his mind.

"Play dumb Joiada" answered Josiah,

"Just tell him you've seen a Star and you believe it could be pointing to the Messiah. Don't tell him you know where it will be, see if he can tell you".

They each thought about the suggestion and mulled it over for a few moments.

"We are wise men seeking to know" said Meres with a smile on his face.

"I like it, that sounds a good idea" added Ashpenaz,

"Perhaps we could make enquires in Jerusalem first before going to Herod".

"Three of you are Gentiles, you would not necessarily know much about it, only that the Jews are expecting a new King" Josiah said.

"The more I think about it the more I like it" said Joiada, "I could keep in the background as I said before, while you three do the talking".

"I always thought you would make a good servant, I'll be your Master" quipped Ashpenaz.

"We could leave the bulk of our train outside the city, split up and just the four of us go to make enquires" offered Kedar.

It was against everything the way they had been brought up, at all times they should have a bodyguard and a servant with them when travelling.

"I'm willing to risk it, we have said all along that it is in God's hands, I'm sure we will be protected by Him". Meres' quiet voice again put them right.

"My, our new Proselytes are showing great faith" Josiah commented.

Joiada looked at his friends and smiled, he said,

"I'll be Meres' servant", then he agreed with the idea and followed with,

"You three go as Magi, I'll dress differently as an attendant, I can listen to what is said but I will keep quiet, do you agree my Princes"?

"I shall enjoy it very much, getting you to fetch and carry as much as I can" Ashpenaz added grinning all over his face.

His roguish eyes showed how he was enjoying the situation.

They had to laugh at him, Joiada pointed a finger at him but he had to grin with the others.

"You make me very envious, the very thoughts of you seeing the Son of God. Meres is right, I feel that you will be well protected, but in the future I will be satisfied to say I helped in some small way" Josiah answered.

They could tell he really meant what he said, he then added,

"I'm thinking of a prophecy that Isaiah wrote for when the Messiah comes".

They all waited in anticipation to hear what Josiah had remembered,

He said,

"And the Glory of The Lord will be revealed
And all flesh shall see it together" Isa 40, 5

"Of course" agreed Joiada, "Why didn't I think of that one, it makes me tremble to think of being so close to The Lord God".

"Uncle Shadrach would be pleased to know how we are progressing, I should send a messenger before we leave tomorrow to bring him up to date" said Ashpenaz, then as an after thought he added,

"With all we have achieved so far and where Triune is now" he suddenly broke off, then loudly added,

"Oh dear, Triune will have fallen from where he is, I doubt whether he can still see it from his home".

Their journey had taken them many miles further west.

"He would have been able to notice a great change before it went out of sight" exclaimed Kedar.

"I had better go and write a long letter" Ashpenaze made ready to leave them to their discussion then added, "I have enjoyed your company Prince Josiah, perhaps I will see you before we leave in the morning".

"Thank you Prince Ashpenaz, I shall make a point of seeing you all before I continue my journey".

Joiada was much more at ease now they had formed a plan for arriving at Jerusalem. It had taken a load off his mind and he felt his enthusiasm surging back once more.

An hour before dawn they met again to have a quick look at Triune.

However, they were genuinely surprised when Josiah joined them, he also wished to see Triune's glory again before he left.

With being able to pick out Triune without a dioptra, he was determined to follow its course until it went out of sight from where his business would take him during the next few weeks or so.

Caesarea Philippi
a City of Cult Worship

Sinners, wrung with true repentance, Doomed for guilt with endless pains,
Justice now revokes the sentence, Mercy calls you break your chains.
(J Montgomery)

The next stage of their Journey changed their direction drastically, almost due south, just a little to the west, forty miles on would bring them to what was known in the bible as Banias.

The going was a little slower as they began to climb from the plain on the fringe of the Golan Heights.

This direction put them on the southern slopes of Mount Herman.

It's springs from the melting snow-caps, drain down into the papyrus swamp of Huleh and feed the beginning of the River Jordan.

One particular spring gushes out from a cave in a cliff of red limestone.

T.E.Lawrence of Arabia, mentioned it in a letter to his mother.

For centuries amid groves of trees there had been a cultic shrine of the Hellenic Pan.

Before that, Canaanite gods had been worshipped.

Nature had set out the dells and groves placing them almost like fairy dwellings, it is thought to have attracted cult worship for thousands of years.

Herod, in 20 BC. Built a Temple to Caesar Augustus, later still, Philip the Tetrarch rededicated it to himself and Tiberious, hence the name Caesarea Philippi.

It was later thought that near here Jesus asked Peter who he thought he was.

Revelation came to the Apostle and he declared that

Jesus was THE SON OF GOD!

What better place for this to happen, to make such a declaration where other gods supposedly had dwelt for so many years.

Now they were truly in Roman Territory.

A Roman Fort had been established here and soon the four Princes were passing a Contubernium, (squad) of eight legionaries, many more were to pass at fairly regular intervals.

With being in their own territory they moved about as they wished.

Two days after leaving Damascus the Princes found themselves ready to enter the City.

Since Herod had built the Temple to Caesar, coupled with it's natural beauty, it had become a tremendous attraction to Greeks and Roman tourists.

This in turn had warranted a few Inns of various size and calibre to be built in order to deal with this new welcome trade.

Joiada made for one of the establishments where he knew the proprietor well. He also was a Samaritan.

An attendant met them as they rode into the yard and Joiada was instantly recognised, he went to inform the Inn Keeper a Royal Party had arrived.

Unlike Joiada his family had been relocated by the ruling powers over the years but fortune had been kind to him, he was now the owner of quite a reputable Inn.

Joiada had dismounted by the time he came out of the Inn, his eyes lit up with delight as he saw who it was.

"My good friend Apelles", shouted Joiada, "We would like to stay for the night and sample your hospitality. Sorry to say, we must be on our way again tomorrow".

"Prince Joiada" he shouted in delight, "What a pleasant surprise, please come in and let us give you the best food and wine we have".

Joiada introduced his fellow Magi and at once the Inn Keeper gave orders for suitable rooms to be made ready for such Royal Guests.

The other members of their entourage were given appropriate accommodation in another part of the Inn.

It was almost the sixth hour, (noon) and before Joiada left his servant he made arrangements for them to have the necessary instruments ready for them to move along to a quiet place outside the city to study Triune after sunset.

The Royal party settled in their rooms and enjoyed the cuisine offered by Mine Host, who was sorry to hear they could only stay for the night.

All four of them were eager to look at Triune, they almost ran to their mounts when called.

Arrangements for their supper had been made for as and when they returned about one and a half hours later.

They did not have to go very far before finding an ideal place just over a small hillock which helped to hide the City lights, moonlight made it easier for them to set up the apparatus.

As they made their way a fairly large cloud was obscuring the part of sky where Triune would be.

By the time the sky cleared two dioptras were ready set and waiting.

But when it cleared they stood and looked up in amazement.

Without any need to focus with an aid, the Princes and their bodyguards could not believe how prominent the three stars had become since two nights earlier.

The three stars were almost touching, what a spectacle they had suddenly become.

Each star was almost the size of Spica which was the brightest star in that part of the sky.

The difference two nights had made was incredible, they could hardly believe what they saw.

Joiada was the first to speak,

"If Triune should not fall for about six weeks, what will it look like then"?

Kedar was first to plot the position with a dioptra.

"I think it may pass Spica by then", he said excitedly, then added,

"How can three tiny stars grow like that in seven months"?

Kedar was the only one to look through the dioptra, enough could be seen so clearly with the naked eye, but he needed to fix the co-ordinances.

"We need to allow for any anomalies that may occur, with such a change we must be ready for anything".

Meres' voice had a hint of mystery with it.

For almost half an hour they stood with heads pointing up until they began to get a crick in the neck.

The ground was fairly dry so for an hour they made themselves comfortable half lying, half sitting in positions to allow them to gaze at Triune more comfortably.

Just over the little hillock in a dell away from the City, the temperature was about eight Celsius, but their desert clothes allowed for all temperatures.

They were hardened desert travellers.

Now being more comfortable they could enjoy this great marvel as they chatted about how fortunate they were to comprehend that something was taking place that could only be controlled by The Creator Himself.

Joiada suddenly thought of the last prophecy he had read, as he gazed up at the great Triune he quoted from Dan 12,3,

"Those who are wise will shine like the brightness of the heavens, like the stars for ever and ever".

"What a wonderful prophecy, that has made me tingle all over" remarked Meres, "Do you think we might shine like stars"?

"Where did you find that one" asked Ashpenaz.

"I read it in Daniel 12 verse 3, I must have forgotten to mention it before, but looking up at Triune suddenly brought it back to me" replied Joiada.

"I don't think we shall ever be as bright as Triune" added Kedar.

"Just think" said Joiada "We are called Wise Men".

"Wise or not, we are all equal" said Meres.

"Do you think everybody could be wise"? asked Ashpenaz.

"One of our proverbs says,

'*To believe in God, is the beginning of wisdom*". Quoted Joiada

"That's the answer then" replied Ashpenaz, "Everyone can shine like stars if they believe in God".

"Amen to that" exclaimed Joiada.

They each followed with "Amen to that".

However, if the sky had not clouded over and the feeling that very soon it would be pouring with rain, no doubt the Princes would have enjoyed looking up at Triune for a very long time but circumstances forced them to pack up and make for the Inn within the hour.

When they finally sat down for supper they ate almost in silence.

Mine host was a little taken aback, Joiada and his comrades had been so chatty he wondered if something had upset them, he was prompted to ask,

"Is everything to your liking Prince Joiada, can I be of any service to you"?

Joiada looked up, he suddenly realised he and the Princes were once more on cloud nine after witnessing such a phenomenal sight.

"Apelles, everything is fine as usual, we are having to make some important decisions, my friends and I are just deep in thought, our meal is fine thank you".

Ashpenaz and the others nodded in agreement. Joiada thought for a moment and added,

"Perhaps if you are not too busy later you would join us for old times sake"?

This brought a smile to Apelles' face again, he was soon the cheery fellow that greeted them, he replied,

"That is so kind of you Prince Joiada, you can be sure I'll find the time as soon as all the meals are served, perhaps about an hour"?

"We will look forward to that Apelles", answered Joiada.

When the four Princes were alone again he asked them,

"Do you think we could ask him anything that may be helpful to us as we get nearer to Jerusalem".

After a minute or so Meres asked,

"Is it worth asking whether there are likely to be any Roman check points getting into Jerusalem".

"You have a point there, better to find out what the military situation is in advance" said Ashpenaz.

"Better the devil you know" Kedar said.

With the Inn Keeper coming to talk to them it brought them back to reality and the discussion now turned to the attention of their Journey.

Joiada had a favour to ask his friends now they were so close to Samaria, he decided to broach the situation, he asked,

"Would you mind me making a call at our Family Residence, we will be going very close by"?

Samaria was almost on the route but Joiada did not wish to take advantage of the situation.

Kedar spoke almost immediately,

"Of course you will call at home, I want to see your dear old mum, I haven't seen her for such a long time", he said most emphatically.

Meres also agreed,

"We have almost five weeks hopefully so you must have a few days with your family".

"I want a goodnight kiss from your sister Doris" quipped Ashpenaz.

This made them all chuckle, but Joiada had adopted his serious grin as he said,

"Doris has been married for quite a few years".

Ashpenaz squinted a little, he then replied,

"I'm too late again".

"You're too much of a playboy to get married" said Meres in his soft voice.

The others all pointed a finger at Ashpenaz,

"Playboy" they said.

"Don't you start" Ashpenaz replied,

"Uncle Shadrach keeps saying it's time I knuckled down".

It was not very much later before Apelles found he had time to spare, he tidied himself up and made his way to their table.

Joiada saw him coming and stood up to welcome him,

"Bring a chair and sit with us Apelles", he said as he poured some wine out for Mine Host.

"It is indeed a pleasure to have you here Prince Joiada", he took the tankard from Joiada and toasted them,

"May you live for ever my Royal Princes".

Joiada had been mulling over what he should ask to start the conversation.

He began with, "We need to go into the city of Jerusalem Apelles, do we need to get a pass or ask permission from anyone"?

Apelles put his tankard down and replied,

"Although the Romans have the main say they allow the Jews to organise the coming and going, as long as everything goes smoothly, they observe in the background and interfere only when there is a disturbance".

"We don't need a pass then" Meres asked.

"It might be better if you left your camels with one of your attendants, you would mingle better on foot"

Apelles replied. Then with a twinkle in his eye he asked,

"Are you planning to assassinate Herod".

Their little party erupted into such laughter everyone in the Inn turned to look at them.

Apelles put his hand up to the other clients to reassure them it was all in good humour.

"Where ever we go" whispered Ashpenaz

"Every body has it in for Herod".

"As long as he doesn't hear us", answered Apelles also in a whisper.

Joiada was pleased he had mentioned Herod.

"We may have to visit Herod" said Joiada,

"Do we need to go through Roman authorisation first"?

"Is it to do with their religion"? asked Apelles.

"In a way yes" replied Joiada, "We would like to ask whether any of their people study the stars".

"Oh, I might have guessed it was to do with you being Magi, perhaps the best way of broaching that subject would be to start at the Temple and see one of the Priests", replied Apelles.

"Of course" said Joiada, "Perhaps if we ask to see one of the Members of the Sanhedrin he would point us in the right direction".

"I'm sure you will have no need to ask for Roman approval" Apelles assured them.

One of his staff came and apologised that he was needed to deal with the arrival of a group of visitors.

"You've answered our question" Joiada replied,

"Please feel free to look after your clientele".

With that Apelles thanked them profusely and made his way to the door.

Joiada sent for his personal attendant to arrange moving on at dawn.

They retired for the night and very soon the Magi were sound asleep.

When the rain took away their view of Triune the previous night they assumed correctly that it would be still raining the following morning.

Even so they were up and about preparing to be on their way to Samaria as daylight broke.

The hills they now had to negotiate as they continued their Journey, made it somewhat slower than being on a flat plain.

Samaria was forty five miles away and their plan was to stay overnight at Nazareth.

Nazareth

Angels adore Him, in slumber reclining,
Maker and Monarch, and Saviour of all.
(R Heber)

The rain eased considerably and by the time they were half way there it had almost stopped.

At the top of their mind they were hoping the sky would be clear enough for them to see Triune, even for only a brief glimpse they would be grateful.

After finding a suitable place to rest for an hour they had some light refreshments.

A few Caravans still plied back and forth on this road but it was nothing like the traffic encountered after leaving Damascus.

It was nearing the sixth hour, (noon) as the entered the smaller town of Nazareth, although it was still a busy crossroads leading south to Egypt, north to Aleppo, and west to the busy ports along the Mediterranean.

The four Princes had no idea that this town would be where the Babe they were seeking would live and grow up to be The Saviour of the world.

Where he would learn the craft of shaping wood and helping his father to keep his dear mother and younger brothers and sisters.

The Inn was quite busy and the four had to share a large room while their eight attendants roughed it sharing a larger room with twelve other men.

As they were about to sit down for their evening meal Seth rushed in and asked to see Joiada.

He was very excited and was told he could approach the Princes.

"Prince Joiada the sky has cleared, your dioptra has been set up outside".

Joiada immediately went to the Inn Keeper and said,

"Please excuse us Mine Host, we are Magi and my servant has just informed me that the sky has cleared, please allow us time to study an unusual happening in the sky, we will make it worth your while when we settle our account in the morning".

At that the Landlord was only too happy to oblige, within minutes the four Princes were outside following Seth.

A dark area fifty yards away from the Inn, was where their other attendants were ready and waiting as they all stood looking up into the sky.

Automatically the Princes looked up in the same direction and saw Triune so clear, so bright, so magnificent a spectacle, they did not need the dioptra.

Once again they were transported almost into another world, the town had been so alive and busy, but most people were now in their dwellings.

The winter was on its way, the temperature was around five degrees Celsius, this put a nip in the air that kept most people indoors, so only a few were outside to notice that a dozen people were standing in a quiet dark place looking up at the sky.

Why the whole world was not outside looking up at this great manifestation was something beyond them, they could only stand and stare in awe.

However, it was not meant to be for them to enjoy this moment very long, after twenty minutes the rain clouds filled the sky.

"The Lord God is certainly teasing us", said Meres.

"We must be thankful for small mercies" added Kedar.

"Have you thought about when it falls"? asked Ashpenaz.

"Do you think it will fall, or will it disappear"? Joiada answered with a question.

"Wow" exclaimed Meres, "I hadn't thought about it like that".

"You may be right Joiada" added Kedar, "It was new when I found it, but if the Lord God sent it just to Herald His Son, we should be prepared for it to disappear when it has led us to the Babe".

No one made a move towards the Inn, it was as though they expected the clouds suddenly to roll out of sight.

"Do you have a feeling about this particular place"? asked Meres.

They looked at Meres although the clouds had made it quite dark.

"Now you mention it" replied Ashpenaz, "I pick up a very weird and wonderful feeling about it".

"I feel it too" added Joiada, "It has to be this place".

"We shall have to remember that *Nazareth* seemed very extraordinary" said Kedar.

"Seth, you must never hesitate to fetch us like you did tonight, that applies to all staff, whoever it is, let us know anytime we are inside and the sky is clear". Joiada addressed them all but he was sure his Royal friends agreed.

"I was so moved I did not plot the position" said Kedar.

"I'm sure that it has not deviated from its set course" added Meres.

They made their way inside and apologised again to the Inn Keeper.

After supper they asked for wine to be taken to their room in order to discuss their progress.

This adventure had so taken over their lives the Magi Princes felt the need to be alone, away from any distractions of a busy establishment like the Inn.

As soon as they had settled down alone they felt they could unwind just telling each other how they had become so engrossed in their calling, each one of them felt special to have been chosen to undertake this assignment set by the Lord God Himself.

"I don't feel worthy to be going to visit our Lord God's Son" said Ashpenaz.

"I feel the same" replied Meres, "But I don't think we can do anything about it but go and enjoy the privilege of being chosen" he added.

Joiada smiled at them as he looked from one to the other and said,

"Three Gentiles, chosen with me, a Hebrew sinner, all on a mission called by the Lord our God".

As usual they were up and away early the following morning. After only a brief rest half way to Samaria they pushed on to arrive by noon.

Samaria Joiada's Home 'Freedom'.

Veiled in flesh the Godhead see! Hail! The Incarnate Deity!
Pleased as man with man to dwell, Jesus, our Emmanuel.
(C Wesley)

What a mixed history Joiada's birth place could boast of.

The Israelite King Omri bought the hill of Samaria for two talents of silver.

On this hill, he founded and named the city he built there by the same name, obviously Omri's name made it a Royal City.

It became the capitol of the Northern Kingdom of Israel after the Lord God took away the ten tribes from Judah.

That was punishment because Solomon had worshipped the idols of other nations.

The ten tribes however, proved to be no better, and because of their sins eventually they were punished.

Another King named Ahab, is worth a mention, his dwelling was called the House of Ivory.

He filled it with ivory panels and carvings, many of which can still be seen in the Palestine Archaeological Museum at Jerusalem.

The City had a very mixed population after Nebuchadnezzar repopulated it during the Exile.

This most likely is why the Samaritans were classed as a mongrel class of Jews.

But to this day there are a small number of Samaritans who still worship the God of Abraham on their Holy Mountain, Gerizim.

Mount Gerizim is about six miles outside Samaria City.

Thirty years or so later, Jesus stopped near here at Sychar, to ask for a drink of water.

The lady he asked was surprised because she did not expect a Jew to even speak to her because she was a Samaritan.

During the conversation she told Jesus what Moses had said about Mt. Gerizim being more important than Jerusalem, it was where her people worshipped God.

Jesus replied by saying,

"God is a Spirit, and those who worship Him should worship Him in Spirit and in Truth".

It does not matter where we are, we don't need to be in a certain town or city, the Spirit enables us to talk to Our God anywhere in the world. Psalm 139.

As Joiada came in sight of his old home his heart leaped, he certainly knew that he could talk to His God wherever he was.

His Family Estate had been built by his grandfather over a hundred years previous.

Set among orchards and small farms outside the City of Samaria.

As he drew nearer he was wondering what his mother would say because he had not been home for two years.

Queen Mother Sarah was told by her daughter Princess Matred that her son and heir was approaching, his entourage was seen entering the gates and proceeding along the broad pathway to their Stately Home called Freedom.

She did not move so quickly now she was in her late seventies but was standing in the doorway leaning on her cane by the time her son drew level.

Joiada alighted after his camel had knelt for him.

He walked up and bowed to his mother, then rose and went forward reaching down to kiss and embrace her.

"So you haven't forgotten where you live after all", she spoke and looked up into his face, her aged eyes had a tear forming ready to roll down her wrinkled cheek.

Her face slowly lit up with a smile as she held him close.

"As if I could ever forget where my dearest Queen Mother gave me birth" answered Joiada.

He was also trying to avoid a tear.

"I can't see my Ruth anywhere" he whispered to his mother.

"We did not know you would be here yet, she is over at the camel park, two were giving birth and she wanted to be on hand, I have sent for her".

Joiada was happy now he knew why Ruth was not here to greet him.

He continued with "I've brought three Princes to see you".

She turned and looked at them, they were standing close by.

As she looked at them they bowed.

"How wonderful to have my Prince return with three more" she put her hand out to them and said,

"Please come into my home so I may enjoy your company as long as you wish to stay".

She gave a small bow before turning and led them through to a large reception hall.

"Brother Joiada" a voice rang out as he followed his mother, a young lady stood there to welcome them, she had quickly sent servants to have three other rooms prepared besides extra amenities in Joiada and Ruth's room.

"Princess Martred, my favourite sister, you are looking radiant as usual" Joiada answered and he picked her up and swung her round.

"You say that to both your sisters, but it is great to have you home" she replied.

"You haven't got time for that according to your father, he informed us that you are on a special calling from Our Lord God". Queen Sarah said jovially.

Joiada and his three friends stopped still in their tracks, they looked at each other dumbfounded, after a pause Joiada asked,

"The King has sent word of our quest"?

His mother and sister both replied,

"Yes".

Mother followed with "We are praying for a clear spell to look at the night sky".

Joiada's face showed a look of surprise, the other Magi were also surprised, they had not expected Nathan to be so forth coming.

They went to their rooms and refreshed themselves ready to join the family at table.

Joiada hurriedly got ready and called his friends into his room for a quick word.

When the four of them were together he said,

"I must apologise for father being so presumptuous, I did not imagine for one moment that he would be so open about our quest"'

"I'm not sorry that he has let the cat out of the bag" said Meres, "I have been wondering myself about when we could tell the world".

"When we go to Jerusalem we shall have to tell everything we know, we have mentioned it to Josiah, I don't mind the family knowing" said Kedar.

"You know me" added Ashpenaz, "I'm sure the Lord God has sent Triune to let the world know".

Joiada was somewhat astounded but also pleased that they each agreed, especially with what Ashpenaz said, he responded with,

"Words of wisdom from Ashpenaz, I hadn't looked at it that way".

"We keep saying, God is in charge, it must be His will".

Kedar reiterated, "Of course it must be His will".

With a great sigh of relief Joiada led them down the staircase to where the family were eagerly awaiting them.

While they had been refreshing themselves, Joiada's brother Rouben had been called from the stables, he was the horse-breeder and dealt only with that side of the Family Business.

Joiada's other sister Doris was also present, she had been supervising a group of donkeys for one of the Caravansaries.

They both greeted Joiada with a hug.

Around the table sat Queen Mother, Reuben, Matred and Doris when the four Magi entered, mother remained seated, the others stood and gave a small bow as the Princes took their seats.

Suddenly someone came bustling in before they had time to sit and said,

"Please excuse me Queen Mother" she almost shouted and a lovely lady ran up to Joiada and embraced him regardless of protocol.

Joiada took his wife and hugged her, it had been two years since he saw her.

He took her out of the door to continue their embrace as Queen Sarah said, "Oh to be young again, try not to be very long" she looked round and winked at her guests.

A few moments later Joiada came in with Ruth and apologised.

It was about the seventh hour, (one pm) when everyone was seated.

During the meal they chatted about everything except Triune, this was to be discussed later.

Queen Sarah could not wait to retire to a lounge in order to hear all about their project, when she thought her guests had finished their meal she asked them to join her in a more comfortable cosy room.

All stood as she moved and followed behind.

Nine seats were arranged around two small low tables with drinks and fruit laid out.

When seated she asked that two Magi would sit either side her, Joiada, Ruth and Ashpenaz sat one side, Kedar and Meres the other.

"We have gathered father has mentioned The Messiah" Joiada began the conversation as he looked at his mother intently.

Queen Sarah smiled and quoted Isaiah 52,7

"How beautiful upon the mountain are
the feet of those
who bring good news, who proclaim peace,
who bringeth good tidings of great Joy,
who proclaim salvation,
who say to Zion, Our God Reigns."

The Queen added, "Actually it should be 'Your God Reigns', it's my way of telling Zion, 'Our God also Reigns in Gerizim'".

She was of course referring to the Jews at Jerusalem, saying He was also their Lord God, but Sarah also implied He was Lord God of all people everywhere.

"Mother you show me up, I know it is Isaiah but what part I don't know" replied Joiada.

"Father said you were spending time with the scriptures again, and the Princes are helping you, I'm so pleased" she said.

"Might I say how lovely you orated from Isaiah" remarked Meres.

"Thank you so very much" she replied, "If I remember rightly you are Meres".

She had not seen them together for many years.

"I am Meres your Highness, we are enjoying your scriptures very much".

His fellow Magi nodded and affirmed it.

"When did father's message get here mother"? asked Joiada.

"He wrote the day after you left" she replied.

She then glanced at Kedar, lifted a finger and asked,

"Kedar"?

"Yes your Highness, I am Kedar".

"You found the tiny stars, we are so excited" her voice echoed her feelings.

"I consider myself very fortunate that I happened to be looking at that particular area of the sky, anyone could have seen them" he replied.

"King Nathan also said you were modest" she said, then turned to Ashpenaz and said,

"Ashpenaz, fancy you wanting to study our scriptures, King Shadrach would be surprised".

This brought quite a bit of laughter from the other Magi.

Ashpenaz looked rather sheepish before replying, "My fame has also gone before me, Uncle Shadrach could never believe that I knuckled down to study at the Academy in order to get my Gold Time Star".

The Queen was quite amused, she smiled as she said, "It is so wonderful having you call to see me, how long will you stay"?

"We have planned for five days, then we must leave in order to keep ahead of Triune". Said Joiada.

"In that case you have time to tell me all about it from the very beginning".

The Magi did just that for the following two hours.

Between them they related all that had happened since Kedar first found the new star cluster.

The Queen and her family never uttered a word except to let in a servant to replenish the drinks and fruit juices.

When Joiada affirmed that was all up to date Queen Sarah looked round and said.

"The King added in his long letter that the four of you were very euphoric, and soon after you had been there the same feeling came over him, he said it was almost like being on cloud nine", she paused and added,

"I seem to have caught that certain feeling myself".

Joiada and his friends knew only too well what the King meant, since following Triune they had been in raptures, their lives had been completely transformed.

Queen Sarah sat back for a few moments then commented,

"To think that Josiah happened to be at Damascus and told you about seeing the couple in The Temple" she paused a moment then added,

"That certainly adds credence to Triune heralding The Messiah".

Everyone in the room sat as if spellbound as she looked at each of the Magi in turn. Suddenly she almost shouted,

"I must come out to see for myself when it is dark".

"If and when there is a clear spell after sunset, Seth has orders to come and tell me immediately, we will be delighted for you to join us with any memeber of the household, all will be most welcome" Joiada exclaimed.

Queen Sarah and everyone present said they were looking forward to it.

"You will need to wrap up if you join us outside my dear Queen Mother" said Joiada, "It is quite cool now after dusk".

Reuben hadn't said much but he had shown great interest during their talk, he asked,

"Do we need to use a dioptra Joiada"?

Joiada shook his head and smiled at his brother,

"My dear brother, when Kedar first saw it we did need a dioptra until about two months ago, but now, when the sky is clear, the whole world can see the majesty of Triune".

Queen Sarah and everyone there had never heard Joiada sound so elated, his voice reverberated as he spoke about Triune.

"We hope that Seth will come running in as soon as the sky is clear and you will understand why we feel the way we do" added Kedar.

"We cannot describe how we feel, you have to experience it" said Meres.

"I never ever thought I could be so fortunate to be chosen by our Lord God" exclaimed Ashpenaz.

Queen Sarah could not believe that even Ashpenaz could have changed so much in such a short time.

She looked at the Magi one by one and said,

"King Nathan was right, you must on a special assignment for our Lord God".

She rose to make her exit and they all stood.

Then she looked upwards and added,

"Please Lord God, may I see Your Glorious Triune".

She walked to the door with her cane, then smiled and nodded as she left the room.

The time had passed by quickly since they arrived, each one retiring to their rooms when suddenly they heard Seth asking for Joiada. It was nearing the twelfth hour, (six pm) as it became dusk.

After being quite cloudy most of the day, Seth had noticed the sky beginning to clear on the eastern horizon.

When Joiada had been informed he told the Magi to be ready.

The Queen was also notified and she immediately prepared herself to go out if called.

By the time the sky had cleared a quarter of the sky the Magi were ready and waiting, setting up in case they were able to record and plot the position. The stars were slowly revealed as the clouds rolled away to the west.

One by one the family and staff began to appear and stand facing the same way as the Magi. When half the sky was clear the Queen was notified, she came out almost immediately with Ruth and all made room for her to stand with Joiada and his friends.

Soon there were about twenty five people all waiting expectantly, some of them did not know just what to expect, they had just been told to come out and watch. One or two went back to get a cloak, it was quite chilly especially with Samaria being on higher ground.

Hardly anyone spoke, they all stood silently.

By the time the edge of the cloud reached the last quarter of sky, it had a silver lining along its edge, the starry sky began to get brighter as if the moon was there, but the Magi knew only too well there would not be a moon for the next five nights.

When Triune was revealed everyone gasped.

All they could do was gaze in awe and wonder as the glorious spectacle lit up the heavens.

After a few minutes the Queen's voice rang out clearly,

"And the Glory of the Lord shall be revealed,
And all flesh shall see it together,
For the mouth of The Lord hath spoken it". Isaiah 40,5

The Queen stood with them for twenty minutes before asking to be excused, Joiada told her she had done well standing out in the cold, she replied,

"I have been transported, It has made me tingle all over, no wonder Nathan said how differently he felt after he had seen the glorious manifestation".

She made her way inside with her daughters.

Another thirty minutes and the sky clouded over from the east.

No one moved inside until the cloud overtook the great starlight that had been revealed.

Joiada was thinking father would be able to see Triune now if he were here.

Jerusalem

Angels from the realms of glory, wing your flight o'er all the world:
Ye who sang creation's story, Now proclaim Messiah's Birth.
(J Montgomery)

Four days later the Magi set off once more as if they were on automatic pilot.

The Princes camel train halted two miles outside the City of Jerusalem on the Damascus Road.

They had come to rest amid a few scattered settlements where a few nomad tents had found open spaces on softer ground.

As the Magi dismounted they tried not to look conspicuous as to their status.

The Princes made their way towards one of the gates while the rest of their consort were to continue on the road but not go through the City.

They were to follow the road round the City Wall to Bethlehem and await one mile further along for the Magi to join them.

Joiada had dressed in the attire of one of his attendants who was nearest to his stature, the other Princes were not going to reveal who they might be until they were in the presence of Herod, assuming he was in residence.

Slowly and carefully, the four of them made their way through the Damascus Gate. It was easy for them to mix in with the hundreds of visitors that thronged the City daily.

Their plan was to make their way towards the Temple Precincts and seek someone to ask about the expected Messiah.

Around the Temple area there were always some teachers of the

Law open to discussion about questions of their belief or the Law of Moses.

After finding a suitable stable where they could leave their camels, they were free to make their way into the Temple Courts.

This great building project that Herod had undertaken had begun in 20 BC, the Temple itself had been completed in eighteen months and was fifteen storeys high. However, the outer court surrounding the Temple was not to be completed until AD 64.

The gate Beautiful leading up from the Kidron Valley would later be covered in silver and gold, it was so heavy, 20 men were needed to open and close it.

Joiada had been on the site before but the other three princes were awestruck by the size of the whole project.

As they moved about they eventually saw one of the priests talking to a small group of strangers, many of the visitors spoke Greek so it was not difficult to pick up what was being said.

They moved closer in order to join the group and stood listening for a moment. Mostly the conversation was about the building of the Temple and it became obvious the priest was not really interested enough to chat about it.

A few moments later he stood alone, he became aware of the three princes, and their servant, no doubt because of their dress, they were very unlike the usual tourist.

"Good day my good sirs" he said, "Can I enlighten you with anything to do with the Hebrew Way of Life".

Meres took the opportunity, he moved closer and asked,

"Could you tell us about your Messiah you are expecting"?

The Priest's eyes lit up and he smiled, he was a pleasant man and welcomed the chance to talk about this particular subject.

"Indeed we are expecting a Great Leader who will come and restore Israel to its great glorious past" the priest said proudly.

Joiada could hardly keep himself from asking questions but he had resigned himself to keep in the background, it should be obvious to the priest he was a servant by his dress and the way he kept behind the others, he could even be taken for a slave.

Kedar was next and came right out with,

"We are Magi, who have travelled from Babylon following a Star sign, we are sure it could be very important to the Jews".

The cat was truly out of the bag!

The priest's jaw almost dropped from his face.

For a moment or two he did not know quite how to answer.

When he had composed himself he tried to keep his voice steady as he said,

"I think my good sirs that you should ask for an audience with King Herod".

In for a penny in for a pound, they hadn't expected this to happen so quickly but now it was all to the good.

Two Temple Guards were asked to escort them to the Palace, at least it proved that Herod was in Jerusalem.

Ten minutes later they were told to wait in the Palace Grounds while his Majesty was informed.

It was almost half an hour later when a Palace Official came to them and asked,

"Are you the Magi"?

"We three" answered Ashpenaz, "This is one of our attendants" he said pointing to Joiada.

"If he stays well in the back ground he may come in with you" the Official said as he eyed Joiada up and down, then beckoning he said, "Follow me".

This they did and entered the Royal Palace with some trepidation as to how Herod would take the news.

They followed through to a large audience chamber. On each side of the doors stood an elite member of Herod's Corp of Bodyguard, both wielding a vicious looking scimitar.

They were very impressive, the sight and size of them made the friends extremely aware they must not upset the King.

The Official turned and said,

"Wait for his Majesty to ask you to speak".

With that the large doors seemed to open automatically and they were led through to the audience chamber.

Herod sat on a splendid throne, four steps led up to the dais on which the throne was set.

The princes were used to protocol but at this very moment they felt very levelled. Indeed they were quite subdued.

Meres as usual thought about the situation they found themselves in and suddenly was given not only the courage, but exactly what to say.

Herod addressed them.

"I have been given to understand that I am in the Presence of Magi, do you have The Gold Time Star".

"Indeed My Lord King, three of us received the Gold Time Stars at The Accademy of Alexandria".

They promptly produced their credentials.

"I am impressed, three Wise Men in my audience chamber", he smiled a wry smile at them,

"It must be important for you to wish to speak to me".

The Official spoke,

"Your Majesty they were asking about the expected Messiah".

Herod looked a little puzzled, it must have been quite a while since someone had spoken to him about the great expected leader the Jews were hoping would come to restore all their lost glories.

Herod had adopted the Jewish Faith but he could not boast that he was Jewish. He was of very mixed parents, but because of his connections with Rome he was their puppet King over Judea.

After a moment, he looked at them and asked.

"Have you seen a sign among the stars"?

"We are Magi who have travelled from the east to seek the one who has been born The King of the Jews, your Majesty" answered Meres.

Herod's face changed in a second.

Meres regretted his statement immediately and that he had not been more tactful.

Herod glared at them, his face was like thunder.

After what seemed like an age, without saying a word, he promptly stood up, climbed down two steps to a second platform level and disappeared to the left.

Each side of the throne were large ornate curtains, they shielded his exit into a side room. This news had shaken him to the core, it was obvious to the Princes he had difficulty controlling himself.

Around the Audience Chamber were at least a dozen well armed elite bodyguards.

Most of his soldiers were paid mercenaries who would not flinch at carrying out any of the Kings commands.

The Princes stood close together not daring to speak. As they stood in silence they wondered whether, if they were arrested to give up easily or to protest.

It was obvious if they tried to resist they could be chopped down in seconds.

Never before had they been in such a hopeless position.

No one spoke. They waited with bated breath.

What seemed like hours, although it was only half an hour, a figure appeared from behind them, he was smiling as he entered, this put them at ease straight away.

Joiada instantly recognised him as The High Priest. He addressed them,

"His Majesty sends his apologies to the Royal Princes, before you arrived he had receive some distressing news and it suddenly overcame him. If you would please follow me we can discuss your star find further with the Council".

With that he turned and asked them to follow him.

They were taken along a corridor into a large room where there were twenty or so Jewish Elders of the Sanhedrin waiting to receive them.

Half of them sat at a large table, the rest stood behind in groups.

Three chairs had been placed facing them and the Magi were invited to sit down.

Joiada of course stood behind as his fellow Magi took their seats.

The High Priest himself sat in the centre with the Council, he said,

"Perhaps my learned visitors would address the Council and state the purpose of your visit".

Kedar had admired his friend Meres for coming straight to the point with Herod so he thought 'it's no use beating about the bush, here goes', he said,

"We have come to ask, 'where is the one who has been born the King of the Jews"?

It was now the turn of almost every member of the Council to be shocked at the news, the High Priest frowned and mumbled,

"King of the Jews".

Kedar continued, "We have seen his star in the east and have come to worship Him".

Now it was obvious,

"When Herod heard this he was disturbed and all Jerusalem with him.
When he had called together, all the peoples Chief Priests and teachers Of the Law". Matt 2

The council immediately went into a discussion among themselves, they were truly in a quandary.

Herod had 'asked them "where the Christ was to be born".

The High Priest rushed off with a few of the Council to give Herod the answer,

"In Bethlehem of Judea, for this is what the Prophet says,
'But you Bethlehem Ephrathah,
Though you are small among the clans of Judah,
Out of you will come for me one who is ruler of Israel".
Matt 2

While the Magi waited they knew that anything could still happen, although they did not feel as threatened as they had done earlier, they were not out of danger yet.

About twenty minutes later they were surprised by seeing the High Priest return and appear to be in a much more genial mood. He smiled as he said,

"King Herod wishes to see you privately in his quarters, please follow me".

The High Priest spoke so quietly they guessed he did not wish any of the other Members of the Council to know.

They followed him along passages, through various rooms until eventually they were beckoned into a small anti-room. They began to wonder whether at any moment armed men would come in and pounce on them, or even something more sinister.

However, when the King himself came in alone, with only him and the High Priest and closed the door behind them they were even more taken aback.

'Then Herod called the Magi secretly and found out from them the exact time the star had appeared.

Herod asked,

"Tell me my learned friends, when did this star appear"?

The four Princes could not believe the difference in Herod's voice.

But immediately they felt relieved, the threat had gone, or so it seemed.

Meres gave the information Herod had asked for, he hoped that at last they were doing right.

"My Lord King, early in the month of Sivian, (May) my friend and I were observing the stars from the old observatory in Babylon. It was my colleague Kedar that noticed in the Constellation of Leo Minor there were three very small new stars".

Herod looked so serious when he heard what Meres had explained, he said softly,

"Go on tell me more".

The Magi were so astounded with the change in the King's attitude, it made them feel more relieved by the minute.

Meres continued, "Since then your Majesty the three stars are now very bright and are heading towards another very bright star. We believe that by the time they fall in the western sky it will be quite an occurrence".

Herod's jaw dropped, his mouth wide open, he said,

"And you believe it heralds the Jewish Messiah".

"It must be pointing to something very special your Majesty" Ashpenaz could not keep quiet any longer.

Herod turned and looked at him for a moment, then asked,

"Was it you who found it"?

"No your Majesty, it was our fellow Magi, this is Kedar" Ashpenaz said.

Herod looked at Kedar and asked,

"Will you call it Kedar"?

"I'm not worthy enough to call it after me your Majesty" said Kedar humbly.

"We have a humble Magi, no doubt you will find a name for it" Herod said with a smirk, perhaps he was hoping to have a star named after him.

"And you have travelled all the way from Babylon"? Herod asked.

Ashpenaze answered,

"Yes my Lord King, my uncle, King Shadrach was quite sure the stars were very special".

Herod again looked surprised and said,

"So King Shadrach is your uncle, I have heard of your uncle, he is a very eminent Magi".

King Herod sat pondering a moment looking up in the air, the Princes almost seemed oblivious to him, they began to wonder just what he was thinking.

Suddenly he gave them the impression of coming back to his senses as he said very quietly, almost as if he did not want anyone else to hear him,

"Go and make a careful search for the Child"

He paused and put his finger in the air and added secretively, "As soon as you find Him, report to me, so that I too may go and worship Him".

The Princes again felt a sigh of relief.

Surely if Herod was asking them to do this, everything would be well.

"We will be only too pleased to report back to you my Lord King" answered Meres and he automatically made a little bow to the King.

This in turn prompted the other Princes to do the same.

With that Herod suddenly turned and left them in the little room alone with the High Priest.

The High Priest looked rather stunned for a moment, but then he also left them.

The Princes were left standing alone in silence as they looked from one to the other, but very soon afterward one of the Council Members came in and informed them,

"King Herod wishes you to continue on your Journey and looks forward to your return, if you follow me I will show you the way out".

This was a tremendous relief to the four Magi, they could not believe they had been dismissed. They followed through what seemed like endless passages until eventually they found themselves standing in the courtyard.

The Member of the Sanhedrin bade them to continue on their way and have a good Journey.

Without saying a word the Princes did not run, but they moved as quickly as they could toward the stable where they had left the camels.

Silently they led their mounts through the City Wall where they found themselves almost alone.

They mounted in silence and rode towards Bethlehem at a steady pace.

Eventually Joiada said,

"I'm very pleased to be out of that place, and I'm sure you feel the same way". He glanced behind furtively almost expecting to be followed.

The others did the same.

Not until the City was well out of sight did they begin to feel safe.

They continued until they saw a signal from a lantern ahead.

A few moments later they were welcomed by their very relieved bodyguards and attendants.

It was very obvious they were very comforted to see their Princes safe and sound, all was packed ready to move.

"We need to move off the road and find a place to camp for the night" said Joiada.

"I seem to remember my Prince" replied Seth,

"There should be a suitable place among those hills to the right".

With that he began to pick his way off the road as he led them to gradually climb into the hills.

The sky was murky but they were all experienced at trekking almost in the dark, their mounts were most reliable enough to find their footings as they left the road in case they were being followed.

When Seth had reached a favourable spot a quarter of a mile in among the hills he stopped and let them gather round him.

"What do you think my Lord, will this be a safe place to halt"?

"There didn't appear to be any other travellers as we left the road" commented Ashpenaz.

Joiada turned to their body-guards, he wanted them to be happy with this place.

They all agreed, two of them insisted on doubling back a little way to make sure no one was following.

The mounts were settled for the night while a camp type meal was prepared.

Not until their scouts returned did they light a small fire among some rocks where it could not be seen.

Camp food was usually cakes of dried figs, raisins or dates, bread had been saved from the previous day to have with goats milk cheese.

Without saying, all talk was almost a whisper, when the four of them had finished eating, they made themselves comfortable half lying, half sitting against a small hillock.

The attendants would take turns to be on watch in twos during the night, they were given orders for a morning call an hour before dawn.

It goes without saying, within minutes the four of them were sound asleep.

However, almost two hours before dawn they were woken because the sky had suddenly cleared so much the stars were brightly shining.

As each one of them looked they automatically turned to look up towards the western sky where they knew Triune would be.

When they saw it they knew why they had been woken earlier, up in the clear sky close to the western horizon, Triune shone down from the heavens giving as much light as a full moon.

'After they had heard the King, they went on their way,
And the star they had seen in the east went ahead of them.'

Every one of them, Princes, bodyguards and servants could not believe their eyes, quite a few minutes passed by before Kedar said,

"I know I keep saying it but how could three little stars have grown into such a spectacle since I first saw them".

"The whole world must be looking up at it now" said Meres.

"I wonder whether father is looking" said Joiada.

The three stars were so close they looked almost as if they were one.

"Even with his tired old eyes he would be able to see such an occurrence as this" added Ashpenaz.

But suddenly after another few moments the sky clouded over they knew they would not see it again till after the next sun down.

"God is still teasing us" Ashpenaz remarked,

"We are allowed to see the wonder of it just long enough to keep us on track, but not too much to hinder our progress".

"Well said" answered Meres,

"You must be right because I could have looked up at it for ever, perhaps two more days and it will be falling from view, we must be close to fulfilling our mission".

"How true, perhaps our Lord God did not wish us to sleep too long, he is pushing us on"! Joiada exclaimed.

Their attendants had been listening, without being told they suddenly became a hustling, bustling group of men bent on preparing breakfast, feeding and loading the animals ready to move on.

"Not only has it spurred us on but if you three are like me, all tiredness has gone" said Joiada as he joined in with packing his gear.

"You are so right, when we settled down last night we must

have all been shattered" added Kedar.

"Renewed energy" Meres retorted, "What a wakeup call".

"What I find difficult to accept is, if you three were as scared as I was when we were in the Palace, I have forgotten all about it"

"Without doubt, we were being protected all the time we were in Herod's clutches, we were safe among all his henchmen".

Meres exclaimed as he stowed his blanket.

Joiada looked from one to the other as his attendant came to say breakfast was ready.

"I am amazed how you three have come to say how our Lord God is looking after us" Joiada said, and added,

"It seems we were not followed, but Herod won't leave it long before he wants to know whether or not we have found the Babe".

"I'm sure he doesn't wish to go and worship Him" Meres remarked.

"We will never forget that look of hatred on his face" said Kedar,

"I understand now the terrible reputation he has".

Joiada chuckled loudly as he added,

"Now you all know why I wasn't looking forward to seeing him".

"You don't think he recognised you then"? Ashpenaz asked.

Joiada laughed again as he said.

"He was too shocked, in any case, he wasn't interested in servants, if I had gone as a Magi he might have taken more notice of me".

They did not waste much time eating and were soon picking their way back to the road leading to Bethlehem.

They set a moderate pace not knowing quite what would happen at their final destination.

Everything had pointed to Bethlehem being the conclusion to the greatest adventure of a lifetime.

There were only four miles from finding where The Son of God was leading them after travelling such a long Journey.

"How should we go about finding Him"?

Joiada asked as they rode side by side.

Very few other travellers were on the road, some carrying a few vegetables or a few oranges to sell at the local market to help with their meagre existence of life.

No one would ever have dreamt that they were bearing gifts for the Greatest King of all mankind.

"Just talk to the locals" Meres answered.

"Should we four go into town alone", asked Ashpenaz.

"It would be less obtrusive. If we go in such a large group we shall attract a lot of attention" replied Kedar.

"How about we split into three groups, a little space to separate us" Joiada suggested.

"That's a good idea" said Ashpenaz, "I wouldn't think we need a bodyguard with us".

"We've proved that we already have one without our escort" said Meres with a smile.

SKETCH OF DOLL IN
STONE MANGER AT
BETHLEHEM

Bethlehem

Shepherds. in the field abiding, Watching o'er your flocks by night,
God with man is now residing, Yonder shines the Infant light.
(J Montgomery)

They halted for a moment and arranged the groups. When they set off again the Magi went first, bodyguards a hundred yards behind them, followed by the servants and pack animals.

Very soon they were approaching Bethlehem, its name translated is 'House of Bread'.

Not only was it King David's birthplace, it was filled with biblical history, now often called the 'Place of the Star'.

Rachel, the wife of Jacob was buried close by, Boaz and Ruth lived here.

There is a well, known as the 'Well of the Wise Men', where tradition has it, the Magi stopped to refresh themselves.

As the Magi approached the town they saw a shepherd watering his sheep at a roadside well.

They decided to stop and give their camels a drink. After alighting Joiada greeted the shepherd.

"Greetings sir, may we give our animals some of your refreshing water".

"Please do so good sirs" he replied,

"Are you just passing through"?

"We have come to see the Town of Bethlehem, it is where so many great people were born, for many years now we have worshipped the God of Abraham, and have travelled from far away to see this place".

159

Joiada thought the shepherd was most likely to be local. If so, he may be able to help with their quest.

Meres now joined them, as usual he decided to get right to the point and said,

"We were told the Jewish Messiah would come from here, do you think that is true"?

The shepherd stopped in his tracks, he had been emptying the water bucket into the stone trough.

He almost dropped it.

It took him a moment to recover himself and answered,

"Have you come because of the Prophecy of Micah"?

Joiada answered immediately,

"Yes, that is precisely why we are here, we have journeyed all the way from Babylon".

The shepherd looked very bewildered, they could see he was thinking just how to answer them.

He finished watering his sheep in silence.

Meres wondered if he had been too abrupt, perhaps he should have waited before talking about the Messiah.

As soon as the shepherd was ready to move off he turned and said,

"I live with other shepherds in the fields near here, I'll have a word with them and ask if they might be able to help you".

With that he suddenly turned and walked away, his sheep following close by.

The shepherds name was Jesse.

He walked away with his sheep at a faster pace than he usually went. He was not sure what to say to these strangers so he was going to tell his friends about a group of strangers asking about the Messiah.

The fact of the matter was that all the shepherds knew a great deal about the Messiah, but he was not going to say anything about it until he had talked with his friends.

If they decided to come and meet the men who had come from a far off land he would find them at dusk, after all he thought, there was safety in numbers.

Kedar watched Jesse walk away, he had heard the brief conversation but somehow he had the sensation that he would see Jesse later.

"There must be an Inn, let's go and talk to some of the locals, that will be a good place to begin with" he ventured.

They led the camels through the town watched by a few women carrying pitchers and children playing near by.

Ashpenaz asked a man leading a donkey where the Inn would be and following his directions they soon stood outside quite an impressive establishment.

An attendant met them and took the reigns of the camels and shouted for an assistant to lead them to the stables, he then led them into the Inn.

After entering they were met by a very jovial landlord.

He came brusquely to greet them, it was obvious he was happy to get some clientele, his trade had been very sparse for many months.

Almost a year ago his trade had been a very different kettle of fish.

Crowds of people had wanted to stay at the Inn, he even had to turn some away.

It was when Caesar Augustus decided to call everyone to go to where their family line was first registered.

By doing so he could to take a Census of the population of all the lands belonging to Rome.

It was so very different this year, only a few Roman Legionaries off duty were staying at the Inn relaxing on leave from their duties.

"Good morning my fine sirs, can I get you some refreshments"? he asked.

With the way they were attired made him realise they were most likely rich merchants.

He had caught a glimpse of their camels from inside the Inn, how they were adorned with such refinery.

This was most noticeable to the Inn Keeper even before the Magi spoke.

"Good Morning landlord, we will sample some of your best

wine to begin with then try your food" replied Joiada, he was trying hard to disguise the Samaritan accent he had developed as a boy, otherwise it would be easily recognised by the Inn Keeper.

Mine Host went off rubbing his hands, he had not entertained so many visitors for quite a while.

Just as he was pouring the wine, four more guests walked in.

Obed, Joiada's bodyguard came in with the other three. They sat near but did not show recognition of their masters.

The two legionaries sat talking discreetly to a lady who was gaudily dressed in bright colours.

The Magi were served and the Landlord asked,

"Would you be staying for the night my good sirs"?

"We most likely will be" replied Meres, he had a very different accent used by Joiada.

Ashpenaz followed with "We will know more when we have met with other merchants later".

The Inn Keeper soon realised the four all spoke with a different accent, this gave him the idea they were definitely merchants from different parts of the land.

Perhaps he thought, they would stay a while to discuss their business.

This pleased the landlord greatly, it made him happy to think his trade was taking a turn for the better.

When four more strangers suddenly entered, he could hardly believe his eyes.

After Ashpenaz' remark the Magi thought it a good idea to recognise their servants as the merchants they were expecting.

Ashpenaz rose to meet them and taking his servant's hand, he led them to Joiada, as he shouted,

"Oh there you are Erastus, I'm glad you've found us".

The four servants just raised their eyebrows a little but did as they were told. They found it very amusing being classed as colleagues.

The Inn Keeper was overjoyed.

Twelve guests arriving unexpectedly, he ran off to call for more staff and told the kitchen to expect visiting the market for more fresh food.

The Magi servants were discreetly put in the picture, so they in turn chatted as though talking business.

After they had been served wine Meres said,

"I think I was too hasty talking to the shepherd, do you think I scared him off".

"He certainly knows something about our mission, I had the feeling he did not know quite whether or not to trust us", replied Joiada.

"I wonder whether he is being careful of who he talks to" remarked Meres.

"I wondered that myself" said Joiada, "He was somewhat hesitant".

"Whatever he was thinking worried him, perhaps if he knew he could trust us he would be more open about it", remarked Ashpenaz.

"Let's hope he gets his friends to agree to meet us" added Meres.

"He's the first person not to respond after mentioning The Messiah" said Kedar.

"Wherever we have stopped and mentioned it, the reaction has been the opposite" added Joiada,

"What's so strange, of all the places I would have thought, Bethlehem to be '*the place*" to create a much more positive response.

"Very strange, I entirely agree" replied Meres.

They decided to wait until they met the shepherd again with the hopes of being able to find him.

"You found the wonderful Triune, leave it to Our Lord God, I'm sure the shepherd will show up again" Joiada assured them.

Meres had been wondering whether they had appeared a threat to him, so he proposed,

"Just the four of us, if we go with our entourage he will wonder just what we have in mind".

"Of course Meres, you have a good point there" Ashpenaz agreed.

With clouds around it began to get dusk just over two hours later, only a few snatches of the sun had appeared all day. A few scatted showers had dampened the ground but no heavy rain had fallen.

When they informed the Landlord they would be staying the night with their fellow merchants, he could not believe his good fortune.

"I'm so glad my good sirs, I've not had much trade recently, now almost twelve months ago I was so full I had to turn people away. My wife felt so sorry for one couple she let them shelter in the stable, the lady was expecting a child".

Joiada looked up immediately and asked,

"Had they travelled very far"?

"From Nazareth I believe", he replied.

The four Princes looked at each other and almost shouted,

"NAZARETH"!

The Landlord looked at them quite startled.

Joiada was dumbfounded, he could not believe it, the hair on the back of his head began to tingle.

The other Magi remembered Joiada talking about the couple going to register for the Census, and how he and Ruth had took pity on them.

"What happened to them" asked Joiada.

The Inn Keeper looked rather taken aback with Joiada asking so many questions about the couple his wife had took pity on.

"They were a very special couple" responded the Inn Keeper, then continued, "My wife helped to deliver their Baby, when she came back later she was so moved by the experience she could hardly speak about it".

"Was that the first time she had helped a mother in that way" asked Meres.

The Landlord lifted his eye brows, he was surprised at the interest being shown about the couple who had sheltered in his stable.

"Over the years my wife has helped to deliver babies so many, many times, that's why we could not understand". Then he added,

"There was something very exceptional about this mother".

With that he went to attend to some other customers who were shouting for him.

The Magi looked at each other, they each had the feeling they were very close to accomplishing their great mission.

"We must get him to tell us more" Joiada said.

"Perhaps when he's not so busy later he will be able to talk again" answered Meres.

They enjoyed the meal set by Mine Host, later when they had chance to ask him, Joiada said,

"Please join us for a drink when you have a moment, we would like to hear more about the couple and their Baby".

It was almost two hours later before the Inn Keeper found time to spare, when he did come over for a well earned rest he sat down next to Joiada.

He had served them with good quality wine, Joiada poured some and offered it to him.

"Please stay and talk to us my friend, you have looked after us well, enjoy some of this excellent wine with us"

Joiada lifted his tankard and toasted him, "Your very good health sir".

The Magi also toasted him, he was so bewildered this gave him the impression they were indeed, very special customers.

After taking a good swallow he looked at them and asked,

"Are you really merchants?, I feel something very unusual about being in your company" he did not quite know how to put it, then asked again,

"This is connected to the couple with the Baby isn't it"?

They could not believe how he had sensed this was indeed the very reason.

"We must tell him who we are" said Meres.

The Landlord looked from one to the other, he was staggered with Meres' statement.

Kedar followed with,

"I'm sure we can rely on this good gentleman not to tell anyone for the time being who we are".

Kedar looked straight at the Inn Keeper and said,

"Can we trust you not to give us away yet? You will be able to at a later date, and it could well be to your advantage".

Mine Host just sat there.

His eyes seemed to grow wider and wider by the minute.

"Tell him Ashpenaz" Joiada thought they could now say who they were.

"We are Magi, Merchant Princes from far away, Kedar here" Ashpenaz pointed to his colleague, "Saw a new group of stars, we thought they heralded something special, we have followed the stars all the way from Babylon to Bethlehem".

The Inn Keeper began to shake.

Joiada took him by the hand to reassure him and said,

"We can understand that you maybe mystified and find it difficult to understand, but don't be alarmed it is to do with someone very much out of this world".

When the Inn Keeper found his voice he managed to croak in a whisper,

"The Messiah".

Now it was the Magi's turn to be bemused.

After a moment Meres asked,

"How do you know it concerns The Messiah"?

"It all comes back to me about the Babe in the stable, when did you first see the stars"?

Kedar replied,

"We first saw them in Babylon eight months ago, but how did you know it was The Messiah"?

A few minutes elapsed before anyone spoke, then the Inn Keeper found his voice again. He sat looking down at the floor as he replied,

"That was a night that was, I remember the couple asking for a room, but I was so full up, I had several men in each room, I've never known anything like it before or since, my wife felt so sorry for the lady she took them to the stable just to shelter them for the night".

He looked around, then continued, "Later that night about the second watch, shepherds came down from the fields asking if they could go to the stable", he spoke almost in a whisper.

He began to wonder whether he was making sense or whether or not he was dreaming.

The Magi now began to put two and two together about meeting the shepherd. Joiada asked,

"What made the shepherds come asking to visit the stable at that time of night"?

"While they were watching over their sheep" he paused, " suddenly a great light shone on them out of the sky".

The Landlord paused again, looked at them and added,

"I know it's hard to believe but that is what they said, they still talk about it".

He reached for his tankard and took a long swig of wine, he then looked at them almost as if to say, 'I'm not making it up'.

"A great light from above" said Meres quietly, then added,

"Was it a visit by an angel"?

The Inn Keeper began to look quite relieved now, Meres' question had put him at ease, he smiled and answered.

"Yes, ------ how did you know"?

"Since we have followed the star cluster we know that the Lord God has led us to visit the Babe".

The Inn Keeper was a Jew, but not a very devout one, but there is something in everyone that fears the Lord in some way or another, he now realised and respected the Presence of God's Son.

"I hope I'm not too much of a sinner my Princes, I did let them stay in the stable".

"Don't worry Mine Host, the Lord God is in charge of everything, he has sent us to Herald His coming to live among us here on earth" Joiada exclaimed.

The Inn Keeper looked happier by the minute, he said,

"They are living in Bethlehem somewhere, the shepherds will know" then he looked longingly at them and asked,

"Can I go and tell my wife? she will be overjoyed".

"Of course" answered Joiada, "You go and tell her how important she was to help that night, but for the time being not to let any other people know".

With that the Landlord left them, he had heard enough to fill him with so much wonder he was so wanting to tell his wife, he rushed off without saying another word.

"We must go and find the shepherds early in the morning" said Kedar.

They all agreed and decided to retire for the night.

However, Seth the faithful servant who had been told to let Joiada know if the sky became clear had organised a watch during the night to keep track of the clouds. Sure enough two hours before dawn the sky began to clear on the eastern horizon.

By the time the Magi arrived outside the sky was half clear revealing the bright stars as the clouds moved towards the west.

They soon realised their objective could not be seen from their present position, the western horizon was hidden by the houses and buildings around them.

They went searching for higher ground until they came to a space known as the field of Boaz.

They hurriedly climbed their way up to the highest part of the field.

As they reached the top of the hill they saw that the shepherds were also there.

Jesse recognised them and shouted for them to come and join his friends.

"This is Adam" he said, "You are very early how did you find us"?

Before another word could be said,

TRIUNE was suddenly revealed by the clouds.

It was almost like daylight, as if the sun had risen early.

The three stars were brighter than Spica, they had moved together so much so, they had became like **One Glorious Star**, the whole of the western horizon was lit up.

'The star they had seen in the east went ahead of them
until it stopped over the place where the Child was.'

Triune was now so low to the horizon, it almost touched a small house.

The house had been built slightly apart from the others.

It looked rather significant, lonely even.

And yet, Triune had enwrapped it in such a glorious sheen it seemed to cry out to the world that it was the most precious house on the whole earth.

The Magi went down on their knees, the shepherds did likewise, every one of them knew that the Son of God, had indeed, come to live with His people on earth.

For twenty minutes Triune blazed down from the sky.

The Magi expected it to slowly disappear below the horizon, but while they had been looking at it, it hung as though it was suspended by the Hand of The Lord **GOD HIMSELF**.

Adam knew his scriptures well, he was reminded of God talking to Job,

He suddenly quoted God's Words,

God said "Were you there,
While the morning stars sang together
And all the angels shouted for Joy". Job 38, 7.

Very slowly Triune began to fade, within ten minutes it had completely disappeared from the sky.

No one spoke for what seemed like eternity, yet it was only minutes after when Kedar exclaimed,

"My STARS have been called home to My GOD".

Slowly, one by one the Magi stood, the shepherds also rose.

Dawn was beginning to break, the eastern sky was getting brighter as the sun made its way through scattered clouds.

Adam, the older shepherd Jesse had introduced before Triune had appeared, was the oldest among the shepherds.

He made his way to Kedar and asked,

"Why did you call them your stars"?

The four Magi smiled at Adam, who looked very puzzled.

"Kedar was the one who first saw the three stars, they were so small you could hardly see them" said Joiada.

"Where did you first see them"? Adam asked Kedar.

"From a very old observatory in Babylon" replied Kedar, his face was a picture, as if he had discovered the whole world.

Adam looked astounded and asked,

"You have followed them all the way from Babylon"?

"Would you come and join us at the Inn, we can talk over breakfast and tell you all about it",

Meres invited them to come and discuss everything between them,

he knew they were all involved.

The Inn Keeper was again surprised when the Magi returned for breakfast bringing with them four shepherds so early in the morning.

They all sat round two tables as the Landlord organised his staff.

"It is obvious to us now where the Holy Babe is, but before we go to visit please tell us your involvement in this great happening" declared Joiada.

"Your Stars were so very bright" said Adam,

"But twelve months ago we saw a much brighter light appear in the middle of the night".

"Brighter than Triune", Ashpenaz almost shouted.

Jesse also could not contain himself, he shouted,

"There was an angel with our bright light".

The Magi looked in amazement at the shepherds.

"You also have played a part in the Birth of the Holy Babe".

Adam explained,

"We were all terrified, it was almost in the same place were you came and joined us, half way through the night.

One minute it was pitch dark, the next minute as bright as daylight".

"No wonder you were frightened" said Ashpenaz.

"The angel comforted us, he told us not to be afraid, he had been sent by God to tell us a Baby had been born" Adam said.

"In a stable" Jesse blurted out.

The Magi suddenly put it all together, the Inn Keeper not having room, his wife taking them to the stable where she helped the Mother of The Son of God.

All that was left now was the most important part of their assignment, going to complete their ADORATION.

"Will you take us to the house"? asked Joiada.

Adam smiled, he also now realised that the Magi were part of God's way of Heralding His Son's arrival.

"Jesse, go and tell Mary and Joseph special visitors are coming to see them within the hour".

Jesse did not need anymore telling, he ran off immediately.

He loved visiting them, the Holy Family also had come to know him very well, he had been the first person to lead the shepherds to worship the New Born King.

The four Princes went to prepare for their visit to see The Son of God.

When they appeared thirty minutes later they looked most regal.

They had dressed themselves as Princes, with the Magi Star showing prominently on their dark blue silk turbans.

Their camels had been brought from the stable.

As they made their way out to their mounts everyone automatically gave a low bow.

What a spectacle to behold as they rode along following Jesse.

Indeed they looked like four Kings on their way to see THE KING OF KINGS.

It was not very far from the Inn, perhaps three quarters of a mile to a higher point of the town, but what a majestic sight.

Jesse could hardly believe he was leading such a Royal Party along the road in his hometown.

The shepherds followed, they also had never thought for one moment that these four visitors were not only Magi, but also Royal Princes.

As they approached the house, they recognised it from how Triune had hovered above it.

When it had appeared with the glorious starlight surrounding it, the house had stood out majestically, but now it looked much smaller, very ordinary.

Jesse went straight to the door and knocked gently.

It was opened by a very average looking man who was dressed rather mundanely.

As he slowly became aware of the magnificent entourage that had come to halt outside his home he could only stand and stare in wonder.

He could not believe that such distinguished riders mounted on camels were the guests he was expecting.

Jesse did not hesitate, he squeezed by Joseph and entered the humble dwelling as the camels knelt for the Magi to dismount.

When he came out again he said,

"Please come inside my Royal Princes".

Although it was on the small side the Magi entered quite easily,

Joiada, Kedar, Ashpenaz and Meres, Joseph had stepped aside then followed almost in a trance.

Jesse stood just inside holding the door open, every one outside tried to look in as the Magi at last came face to face with the BABE they had come to worship.

A very young lady dressed in a blue homespun garment was standing at the side of a very new, well-made wooden crib.

In the crib a small Child watched as they made their way in.

Jesse, still standing in the doorway, said,

"This is Mary and Joseph, and their Son Jesus".

Mary looked at them and smiled as she said,

"You have come to visit My Son".

Joseph was bewildered, he stood in silence at Mary's side.

He couldn't ask them to sit, there were only two chairs, also very newly made.

"We have come to worship THE KING OF KINGS", exclaimed Joiada.

He looked at Mary and said,

"You must be the Mother of Our LORD, please sit down".

Mary showed a sign of recognition, then asked,

"Have we met"?

Joiada replied,

"You had some refreshments with us on your journey to Bethlehem".

Her smile became radiant as she said,

"Now I remember, you were so kind".

"I did not know that I was entertaining the Mother of My Lord and King" Joiada bowed down to the Holy Mother.

The other Magi did likewise.

The four Princes then moved round the crib and took off their turbans.

Kneeling down, they put their faces almost touching the floor to pay homage to the Holy Child.

For quite a few moments they bowed their heads very low in ADORATION TO THEIR GOD.

Mary could only gaze at the scene in astonishment.

Four special Magi Princes had come to bow down and worship her Baby, but Mary knew only too well that HE WAS INDEED MOST SPECIAL.

Joiada spoke first, he lifted his head and looked at Mary then at Joseph as he knelt at the crib, the Holy Child smiled at them, he perhaps thought they were playing a game.

"We have travelled from far away to worship the Holy Child, my friend Kedar first saw His star in the east and we followed it all the way to this house. God showed us the way".

"We have brought gold for a Holy King" said Kedar placing a casket near the crib.

"Frankincense for the Son of God" said Ashpenaz as he placed two caskets near the crib.

"Myrrh for the Son of Man", said Meres placing an alabaster container near the crib.

Mary now sat on one of the chairs, Joseph stood beside her, although she had been surprised when she first saw them, she also knew she was the Mother of GOD'S OWN SON.

Mary spoke,

"An angel came and told me that I would have a Son, he also told me He should be called Jesus".

"Were you aware of the light around your house early this morning" asked Joiada.

"Yes", she said "I did see the light but since Jesus was born so many wonderful things have happened, now four Royal Princes have come with such wonderful gifts for Him".

Joiada realised that it must have been overwhelming for them, Joseph had not spoken, Joiada said.

"Thank you for letting us come in to worship the Holy Babe, we will leave you in peace now, I think we will stay another night at the Inn and leave tomorrow, please let us know if we can help you before we go".

Joiada bowed to the Son of God once more. Then he stood and bowed to Mary and moved towards the door, he turned and thanked Joseph then left them.

One by one the other three princes followed Joiada's movements and followed him outside.

Jesse had stood just inside the doorway and witnessed the whole event, he also thanked Mary and Joseph before leaving.

Joiada was waiting with the other shepherds when he came out.

"We will be glad if you would join us again this evening" said Joiada,

"We can fill in more details of how we came to meet and be allowed to have played a part in welcoming The Prince of Peace to come and live with us".

The shepherds were honoured at being invited once more.

Previously they had believed the four men were just ordinary merchants.

Now they had seen them in their Royal refinery with Magi Turbans they were truly bowled over.

The shepherds were to come along at the eleventh hour, (6 pm) to talk about their adventures together.

Now the Magi had no reason to go out and look at the sky.

Triune had done what it had been sent to do, to Herald God's Son and let many people share his coming to live on earth among His people.

The Princes made their way back to the Inn riding their camels, there was no reason now to hide their identity.

As they alighted at the Inn, numerous people stood watching, many had never seen the likes before as they gazed in awe and wonder.

The Inn Keeper was standing in the doorway, as Joiada led them in he stood aside and bowed.

He was surprised when they sat down dressed as they were for some refreshment.

The rest of their entourage had followed on foot. But now they sat apart from their masters, it was obvious to Mine Host they did not arrive this way in order to hide their identity.

The Landlord approached rather solemnly and said,

"My Lords, forgive me, if I had known",

"Say no more my good man" said Joiada,

"We chose to arrive incognito but it all happened for the best, your Inn and your good wife all played an important part, now we have been to pay homage ourselves, our mission is over, we will stay the night and be on our way early in the morning".

"Oh thank you my Lords, I don't think I shall ever get over it".

Ashpenaze looked at him kindly and softly said,

"We have something to celebrate now, bring us some of your best wine".

Later that evening the four shepherds came to join in with the celebrations.

They listened to each other as they took turns to explain their individual part that had led up to welcoming and paying homage to the Son of our Lord God Himself.

The rejoicing came to an end, the shepherds said they would say goodbye in the morning and then made their way to watch over their flocks by night.

However, the heavenly interceptions had not ceased.

Each of the Magi had rather a disturbing night, all four had a dream that they should not return the way they came, and to avoid seeing Herod at all costs.

"And being warned in a dream not to
Go back to Herod, they returned to
Their country by another route". Matt 2,12.

They were even more surprised when each of them realised they had received the same message directly from God Himself. It further assured them what an important part they had contributed to Lord of Lords.

Likewise Joseph also had a dream.

When they had gone, An angel of the Lord appeared to Joseph in a dream.

"Get up" he said, "Take the Child and His mother and escape to Egypt.

Stay there until I tell you, for Herod is going to search for the Child and kill Him". Matt 2,13.

From such an early age the Christ Child was in danger from certain people He had come to live with, this would be the first of many crises during His Life, after being sent to save all who would love Him.

Well before dawn plans were made accordingly.

Joiada and Ashpenaz went to visit Joseph.

To their surprise they found him loading his donkey, Mary stood in the doorway of their house holding the Christ Child.

Joiada almost knew before he asked,

"You have had a dream"?

Joseph looked very startled, he answered,

"I must go to Egypt and stay there until I'm told to return" he paused and almost croaked as he said,

"Herod is coming to kill Him".

"We have planned how we may help you, I have brought two donkeys for you to ride, use that one to pack the most important things you will need on your Journey".

Joiada's words seemed to bring reassurance to the Holy Family.

Meres and Kedar had retrieved their blankets made of camel-hair and other warm clothing from their gear that would help to keep the Holy Family warm during their journey.

Another blanket had been formed into a rough 'side-saddle' for Mary to ride on, this was the customary way of all eastern women when riding on donkeys.

The Magi servants and bodyguards were busy dividing their animals into two groups.

A pack of dried food was taken to give Joseph at the house.

The Inn Keeper did not ask why the plans had been changed to such an early start, he guessed that somehow it was important for them to be away.

After settling the tariff with the Inn Keeper the two groups followed to the house as it was just breaking light.

Joiada and Ashpenaz with their bodyguards and servants were going to accompany the Holy Child to the Egyptian border and put them in care of a travelling Caravan.

Kedar and Meres were first going south, then east to go round the Dead Sea and then turn to travel north up the King's Highway and on through Petra.

The Magi parted company reluctantly, they arranged to meet at Joiada's home one month later to bring each other up to date.

With that they went in opposite directions, Joiada heading for a small unobtrusive road leading to the hills, their way passed the hill of Boaz.

As they went by in the morning light they were able to see the shepherds waving goodbye.

Bethlehem is over four hundred metres above sea level, as they trekked through the mountains it began to snow, the Holy Party were very thankful of the blankets around them.

The Holy Babe was snug and warm inside his papyrus papoose type basket. His Mother held Him very tightly as they jogged along.

Kedar and Meres slowly travelled along the main road trying to attract as much attention to their departure as possible.

They travelled totally in the opposite direction hoping this would divert attention from the departure of the Holy Family.

Herod's henchmen did come to Bethlehem.

They killed all babies and children living there aged two years and under.

The shepherds realised immediately why Joseph and Mary had made a hasty retreat without saying goodbye.

Adam said, "God has taken His Son out of harms way".

He sat in the warmth of the brazier with the other shepherds, he was thinking about the message that the angel gave to the world,

"Behold I bring you good tidings of great Joy
that will be for all people.
Glory to God in the highest and on earth peace
To whom God's favour rests
MAY GOD'S FAVOUR REST UPON US ALL.

Epilogue

Return to Freedom

King Nathan had returned home to Samaria before the Magi had arrived at Bethlehem.

Now he and his family were eagerly awaiting with baited breath to hear the final outcome of this great escapade that our Lord had predetermined.

Exactly one month after the flight from Bethlehem the four Magi met at Joiada's home.

All had gone well according to plan.

All the people employed on the Estate had been told one way or another about the Magi's assignment to follow the Star of the Messiah.

Everyone was now gathered with the family to hear the conclusion.

All sat in the largest room, younger staff sat on the floor around the family.

Joiada did most of the talking with his friends joining in here and there as the story unfolded.

Everyone listening sat enthralled as they heard the final adventures of the four Magi Princes.

Ashpenaze quietly said to King Nathan,

"I placed your present alongside mine".

Nathan looked at him with watery eyes and replied,

"Thank you so much, I feel honoured that The Son of my God received a gift that I had handled myself".

When Joiada told about Triune's last appearance while kneeling with the shepherds Nathan suddenly stood and shouted out with tears rolling down his cheeks,

"We all saw it", he was so moved with the memory of it he added.

"We were all outside and watched it slowly fade away".

The Magi were surprised, but soon realised that Samaria was almost on the same meridian as Bethlehem, they would have been able to witness GOD'S WONDERFUL PHENOMENON TELLING MANKIND HOW HE HAD COME TO LIVE WITH US.

"Even with my old eyes I saw the sky lit up like a full moon, it was Awesome" Nathan sat down slowly, his whole household had witnessed it all with the King.

He had now been able to see Triune three times.

Joiada could hardly believe all the people gathered in the large room had witnessed God's Miraculous Sign in His Glorious Heavens.

As each member of staff left the room in silence it was obvious they were all quite moved after being allowed to hear how God had let His Son escape out of harms way.

Little did they know that their visit to Bethlehem would later be recorded for all mankind by the Apostle St. Matthew, in what we now know as,

THE NEW TESTAMENT.

Also that it would eventually be joined to the LXX account in Greek, which is our OLD TESTAMENT.

It records the whole time that Jesus lived among us, and how He died among us, and

HOW HE ROSE FROM THE DEAD AMONG US
TO GIVE US EVERLASTING LIFE.

How His followers spread the Good News around the world.
One of them was in Athens one day trying to convince some

Greeks that they could live forever if they Believed and Followed the Son of God.

This is what he said,

"The God Who made the world and everything in it,
is the Lord of heaven and earth and does not live in temples built by hands, and is not served by human hands as if He needed anything, because He Himself gives all men life and breath and everything,
From one man He made every nation of men, that they should Inherit the earth;
and HE determined the times set for them
And the exact places where they should live.
God did this so that all men should seek Him and perhaps
Reach out for Him and find Him,
though He is not far from each one of us.
For in HIM we live and move and have our BEING.
Spoken by St, Paul. Acts 17, 24-28.

Bibliography

Encyclopaedia of Bible Life published 1963 A & C Black
Madeline S and J Lane Millar
This book gave me the inspiration to write the Magi Story.
Study Bible NIV Hodder and Staunton

Software

Ellis Bible Library 7. Ellis Enterprises USA
www wikipedia encyclopedia.